Atlantis in Mexico

By

Dr. Clyde Winters

Table of Contents

Chapter 1

Atlantis in Mexico

"On the contrary, the evidence, although negative, is that the Olmec style of art, and Olmec engineering ability suddenly appeared full-fledged from about 1200 B.C.". Michael D. Coe in Regional Perspectives on the Olmec, (ed.) By Robert J. Sharer and David C. Grove (Cambridge,1989).

Archaeologist are conservative by nature. This makes Coe's statement about the Olmec's sudden appearance in Mexico startling to say the least.

The Olmecs founded the first civilization in the New World. The Olmecs are a mysterious people credited with inventing most elements of the later Meso-American civilizations, including writing, religious ideology and pyramid building.

The name Olmec, for the founders of America's first civilization, comes from the word **olli** (rubber). Most people found in Mexico only knew the founders of Olmec civilization as "the people who live in the direction of the rising sun"[i]. The term Olmec means "Dweller in the Land of Rubber".

The only "historical" information we have about the Olmecs comes to us from the oral traditions of the Maya and Mexica (Aztec) people recorded by the Spanish chroniclers Friar Diego Landa and Father Bernardino de Sahagun. Other information about this mysterious people comes from the Popal Vuh, a historical text by the Quiche Mayan Indians. All of these traditions claim that the Olmec people arrived in Mexico from a land across the sea.

The Olmec according to Michael D. Coe (1989) and Jacques Soustelle (1984) introduced the calendar, government, religious traditions and architectural styles to Meso-America. Commenting on the Olmecs Zecharia Sitchin in the *The Lost Realms* , wrote that: "Of all the lost civilizations of Mesoamarica,that of   the Olmecs is the oldest and the most mystifying. It was by all counts the Mother Civilization, copied and adapted by all the others. It dawned along the Mexican gulf coast at the beginning of the second millennium B.C. It was in full bloom, at some forty sites by 1200 B.C...."(p.97)

Paul Jordan in The Atlantis Syndrome claims that archaeological evidence indicates that the Olmec civilization did not appear suddenly in Mexico. In fact, he claims that this theory has been "long-demolished". Jordan wrote: Atlantologist and other 'alternative archaeology' exponents go on repeating the same hoary and long demolished claims that the Olmecs of Central America…spring into being in the archaeological record without local precedence from whatever 'nowhere' any particular writer favors (p.90).

This is a simple interpretation of Olmec history archaeology. In reality, controversy surrounds the origins of the Olmecs there is no archaeological precedent for the Olmec civilization, which appears suddenly and already, developed.

Some researchers, such as Michael Coe and claim that the Olmecs are the mother culture of Meso-America. Other researchers, like David Grove and Joyce Marcus believe that the Olmec shared ideological perspective with contemporary cultures in Mexico.

Supporters of the continuity hypothesis for Meso-American civilization claim that the Olmecs civilization was descendant from earlier cultures in the Soconusco region. The ancient cultures of Soconusco are referred to as the Mokaya tradition. These cultures include the Barra (or Ocos) phase (c.1700-1500 BC), and the Locona phase (c. 1500-1300 BC) of the Mazatan region (Clark & Pye, 2000).

The art of the Mokaya tradition is characterized by female figurines, fine pottery and fat males wearing animal mask (Clark & Pye, 2000).

Although researchers attempt to link the Mokaya tradition sites with the raise of the Olmec, as you can see from the dates for the Ocos (1700-1500 BC) and Locona (1500-1300 BC) phases. These cultures were in decline by the time of the Olmec arrival in Mexico around 1200 BC. Much of the discussion of continuity between the Mokaya tradition and Olmec culture is based purely on conjecture and speculation. In discussion of this alleged relationship, Clark and Pye (2000) observed that " **The Mokaya's impact on the first villagers of Olman remains to be determined, but we think it was significant**" (p.243). Just because one "think[s]" a relationship "was significant" does not make it so.

The Olmec ceramics date between 1200-950 BC. As a result, Clark and Pye (2000) speak of the Olmecization of the Mokaya tradition. Clark and Pye report that:"The Mokaya appear to have gradually come under Olmec influence during the Cherla times and to have adopted Olmec ways. We use the term olmecization to describe the processes whereby independent groups tried to become Olmecs, or to become like the Olmecs….The final stage of olmecization was the actual presence of Olmecs in the region and a nearly full conversion of local artifacts to Olmec norms " (p.234).

The quote above makes it clear that the archaeological evidence from Mexico, despite claims otherwise, does not show any continuity and succession of Olmec culture, from the cultures associated with the Mokaya tradition.

The Olmec civilization appears to have suddenly appeared in Mexico without any evidence of a preceding culture. Commenting on the origin of Olmec civilization, Carolyn Tate of Texas Tech University wrote that:"Olmec culture as far as we know seems to have had no antecedents; no material models remain for its monumental constructions and sculptures and the ritual acts captured in small objects. The primal power of the art style springs partly from this lack of formal precedent" (p.65).

Controversy surrounds the exact date for the Olmec civilization. Archaeologists believe that this civilization lasted from 1200 to 100 B.C. Other scholars believe that the Olmec civilization lasted up until A.D. 600. They built beautiful plazas in front of their temples where they placed carved huge heads 8 feet high, painted black and weighing tons.

Ivan Zapp and George Erickson, in Atlantis in America noted that the Olmec heads show African people, with kinky beards and braided hair. Today we have a total of sixteen colossal heads: one from Hueyapan ,three from Tres Zapotes, eight heads at San Lorenzo, and four heads from La Venta. Although each head has a different helmet ,all of these heads show heavy "African" features. Other examples of these Africans are found on thousands of bas-reliefs, sculptures ,statuettes and stone carvings.

The art of the Olmecs is characterized by large stone monuments, especially the well known heads of the Africoid rulers of Olmecland that have striking features similar to the rulers of the 25th Dynasty of Egypt. This is not surprising because the Manding people, that formed the base of the Olmec people, and the Kushites that founded the 25th Dynasty, originated in the Fertile African Crescent, before they spread into Nubia, West Africa and ancient America. The Olmec giant heads, which are almost identical to the 25th Dynasty type, have been found at La Venta and San Lorenzo. In addition to monumental art the Olmec personal art includes human figurines, ceramics, small stone sculptures, masks and axes.

The Olmec civilization has been found throughout much of Mesoamerica. They were accomplished artists, engineers and scientists. They constructed elaborate pyramids and large sculptured monuments weighting tons. There efficient agricultural practices supplied them with an abundant food

supply, which was used to support their large and highly
developed society.

The Olmec civilization appears to have suddenly appeared
in Mexico without any evidence of a preceding culture. The first
scholars to discover the first giant head of an Olmec Jose Maria
Melgar y Serrano[ii] , in 1869 writing the Bulletin of the Mexican
Geographical and Statistical Society , noted that:" As a work of
art, it is, without exaggeration, a magnificent sculpture...but
what amazed me was that the type it represents in Ethiopian. I
concluded that there had doubtless been blacks in this region,
and from the very earliest ages of the world "[iii].

Intensive research into the Olmecs did not begin until
1939, when Dr. Matthew Stirling discovered one of the huge Olmec
heads at Tres Zapotes. At the time of its discovery he wrote:
"Cleared of the surrounding earth it presented an awe-inspiring
spectacle. Despite its great size , the workmanship is delicate
and sure, its proportions perfect. Unique in character among
aboriginal American sculptures, it is remarkable for its
realistic treatment. The features are bold and amazingly Negroid
in character."[iv]

Controversy surrounds the exact date for the Olmec
civilization. One group of scholars believe that this

civilization lasted from 1200 to 100 B.C. Other scholars believe that the Olmec civilization lasted up until A.D. 600.[v] The Olmecs built beautiful plazas in front of their temples where they placed carved huge heads 8 feet high, painted black and weighing tons.

Today we have a total of sixteen colossal heads: one from Hueyapan ,three from Tres Zapotes, eight heads at San Lorenzo, and four heads from La Venta. Although each head has a different helmet ,all of these heads show heavy "African" features, first noted by Matthews and Melgar. Other examples of these Africans are found on thousands of bas-reliefs,scultures ,statuettes and stone carvings.

Although Dr. Stirling, when he first discovered the Olmec heads at La Venta, and Mr. Melgar felt that Africans had early colonized Mexico, most if not all contemporary Meso-American archaeologist refuse to seriously regard the colossal Olmec heads as representing Africans. Although the Africoid somatic traits of the Olmec colossal heads astonish most archaeologists, these Eurocentric scholars maintained that Africans did not arrive in America until the Atlantic slave trade.

Many researchers have recognized many analogous features between the Olmec and African civilizations. Leo Wiener, in

Africa and the discovery of America , believed that the duck billed Olmec statuette from Tuxtla had been inscribed inscriptions used by the Manding people of West Africa. R. A. Jairozbhoy, in Ancient Egyptians and Chinese in America, recognized an Egyptian influence among the Olmecs. Ivan van Sertima, in They came before Columbus, found many features among the Olmecs that suggested a Nubian influence in Mexico And Alexander von Wuthenau, using hundreds of photographs of ancient Olmec works of art in The art of terracotta Pottery in Pre-Columbian Central and South America, illustrated that both Semitic and Egyptian types lived among the Olmecs.

The African Colonies of Atlantis

The Olmec people were descendants of the Atlanteans that formerly lived in ancient Libya. People from numerous ethnic backgrounds , including Europeans, and Semitic types in addition to Africans lived among the Olmecs. Although all these scholars recognize an African influence over the ancient Olmec civilization, they have not been able to pinpoint the exact location for the dispersal of the Olmecs from Africa to Mexico. This results from the fact that these researchers have failed to understand that the Olmec culture is analogous to that of Egypt and Nubia, because the ancestors of the Olmecs , were people from the ancient Sahara, or Fertile African Crescent, before it became a desert.

Although all these scholars recognize an African influence over the ancient Olmec civilization, they have not been able to pinpoint the exact location for the dispersal of the Olmecs from Africa to Mexico. This results from the fact that these researchers have failed to understand that the Olmec culture is analogous to that of Egypt and Nubia, because the ancestors of the Olmecs , Egyptians and Nubians all came from the Fertile African Crescent. The Fertile African crescent was situated in what the ancient scholars called Libya, which was a colony of the **Atlateans**.

The information we have about Atlantis , comes from the Greek philosopher Plato, in his dialogues between Socrates (his teacher) and Timaeus, and Critias (Plato's grand-father) and Hemocrates. in Plato's Timaeus , we learn that Libya was part of Atlantis. He wrote that Atlantis "...controlled within the strait, Libya up to the borders of Egypt and Europe as far as Tyrrhenia". (Spanuth 1979, p.269)

The Atlantis civilization was intimately involved with ancient Libya, which was the name applied to Africa. This is supported by the fact that the first king of Atlantis, according to Plato in Critias, was Atlas. It was from, according to Plato that the "island [Atlantis] and surrounding Ocean took their designation of 'Atlantic'..."(Spanuth 1979, pp.272-273).

The Fertile African crescent was situated in what the ancient scholars called Libya, which was a colony of the Atlateans. Today the Sahara is a desert. Colin Wilson and Rand Flem-Ath in The Atlantis Blueprint , discussed the mysterious ancient civilization that formerly existed in the Sahara that made exquisite pottery and glass in an ecological system rich in flora and fauna.

The possibility that the Olmec civilization is a product of the neo-Atlantean's genius is supported by Plato who noted that the island of Atlantis ruled Africa as far as the border of Egypt. Moreover, although Atlantis was situated behind the Pillars of Hercules, in the Atlantic Ocean, it also had control of territories west of Atlantis. These territories west of Atlantis may be an allusion to Mesoamerica.

The colonization of the Sahara by Atlanteans is supported by the Greeks and Romans who called the inhabitants of the Fezzan and Bilma: **Atlantes**. The literary testimonies of the ancient writers is supported by archaeological data we will discuss later that support the view that the Egyptians came from the Sahara, before they invaded the Nile valley and formed the Egyptian civilization.

The original inhabitants of the Sahara where the **Egyptian** civilization originated were Atlanteans. These Atlateans formerly lived in the highland regions of the Fezzan and Hoggar until after 4000 BC. This ancient homeland of the Dravidians, Egyptians, Sumerians, Niger-Kordofanian-Mande and Elamite speakers is called the Fertile African Crescent. (Anselin 1989,pp.16 ; Winters, 1981,1985b,1991). The ancients called these people Atlateans. (Winters 1985b,1991) The generic term for the African branch of the Atlanteans was **Kushite.** I. Donnelly, in Atlantis: The Antediluvian World, wrote that "The [K]ushites and Ethiopians, early branches of the Atlantean stock, took their names from their sun 'burnt' complexion; they were red men."(p.194) We will call the Libyans, neo-Atlanteans because they did not live on the island of Atlantis.

Francois Lenormant in Manuel d'Histoire Ancienne de l' Orient , insisted that the human race and civilization issued from **Upa Merou.** This view was supported by the Greeks who claimed that "men sprung from **Merou**". Theopomus tells us that the people who inhabited Atlantis were the **Meropes,** the people of **Merou**. This name Merou, of Lenormant and Theopomus may refer to the ancient Kushite city called Meroe .

The Atlanteans and neo-Atlanteans were suppose to have lived around a large lake called Tritonis, situated in Libya. (Graves 1980) Lake Tritonis was located in the Libyan Desert. Here as early as 7000 B.C., there was a slow transition from hunting, to cattle pastoralism. The prehistoric appearance of a great lake in Libya has been recently supported by satellite pictures of the Eastern Desert, which indicate that a lake was located in the Qattara Depression of northwest Egypt. MaCauley, et al (1982) after examining pictures of Libya, taken from outer space found that around 10,000 years ago pluvial conditions existed in the Sahara, which led to the creation of numerous riverbeds now buried under tons of sand.

Climate changes in the Sahara have influenced the subsistence patterns in the Saharan zone. (Winters 1985b) This has been especially true in regards to the rainfall pattern. For example, although the Sahara is presently a desert, there has been three episodes of increased rainfall in the Sahara: c.7000-6500 B.C., 6200-5900 B.C. and 5700-3800 B.C. (Barker 1989:35)

During the Neolithic subpluvial (7000-6000 B.C.) farming and herding were practiced by the Atlateans in the green savannas of the Sahara. Migrating neo-Atlanteans took domesticated cattle into the Nile Valley.(Hoffman 1979, p.102) These pastoral people also spread into West Asia and other parts of Africa.

During this pluvial or wet period in the Sahara the Atlanteans popularized boat building. During this period boats were the major means of transportation. Apart from human and animal figures appearing on Nubian rock art, the most dominant motif during this period is the reed boat. Boats of identical design were also made in Mesopotamia and the Indus Valley. The first use of the mast and sails on reed boats, along with cabins on the deck appear at **Ta-Seti**, a country situated in Nubia 5000 years ago. An analogous boat with a cabin has been found on Izapa stela no.67.

Saharan Boats

In the riverine cultures of Atlantean Libya, each community had marine architects, ship builders and expert sailors. The presence of an elevated bow and stern on many boats depicted in the Saharan rock art and the peculiar "bowstring", astern and "fuse" for the rudder oar, indicate these ancient ships were used for navigation on the open seas. Reed or plank boats are still made by the Dravidians in India, and the Bozo of West Africa, who live near the Niger river.

Egyptian Tomb Boats

The goddess of the Atlanteans in Libya was Athena. The goddess according to Greek traditions was born near Lake Tritonis. (Graves 1980, p. 44) The goddess Athena, was called Neith by the Egyptians and Nia by the Manding and Eteocretans (real) Minoans.

The father of Athena or Neith was **Poseidon** or Potidan "he who gives drink, the wooden mountain" or boat (i.e., a boat on the ocean is like a mountain on the sea) suggest that Poseidon. The identification of the trident   , which was held by Poseidon as a symbol of political authority, was adopted by all the succeeding Atlantean civilizations as their symbol of royalty.

This is evident in the fact that the trident, is a identical to the **serekh** of the Egyptians. The **serekh** was the Egyptian sign for kingship. A bird is often placed directly on the top of the Egyptian **serekh**.

The trident or **serekh** was also a sign for royalty among the Olmecs. This **serekh** is found in many of the inscriptions written by the Olmecs and also their monuments.

On the monuments the Olmec **serekh** sign is more rounded than that of the Egyptian style **serekh**. This sign is evident in the mask face from Chalcatzingo Relief 2, and the relief from Chalchuapa; and monument no. 52 from San Lorenzo, the celt from Arroyo Pesquero,Veracruz and the Las Limas figure.(see figures 3 and 4)

The Greco-Roman writers made it clear that the Atlantean civilization in Libya began to decline as the Sahara became a desert. Due to radical tectonic movements a catastrophe occurred which blocked springs that fed Lake Tritonis. The Roman scholar Diodorus, wrote that Lake Tritonis "disappeared from sight in the course of an earthquake when those parts of it which lay towards the ocean were torn asunder". Ovid, another

Roman writer said that the Sahara or Libya, became a desert after Phaethon's conflagration. Ovid, in Metamorphoses Book II, wrote that "Then also Libya became a desert for the heat dried up her moisture".

The advent of hyper aridity led to the collapse of the Atlantean political control in much of the Sahara. High population density, and the resultant need for a reliable food supply forced the neo-Atlanteans to migrate out of the Sahara into other parts of Africa, Asia and Europe.

This climatic shift probably refers to the 4th and 3rd millennia when the Sahara began to become more arid. This aridity set in motion a number of migrations that forced the Atlanteans and their subjects to seek out new areas for settlement.

In the ancient Egyptian hieroglyphs the neo-Atlanteans were called **Ta-Seti** and **Tehenu** . Farid (1985,p.82) noted that "We can notice that the beginning of the Neolithic stage in Egypt on the edge of the Western Desert **corresponds** with the **expansion of the Saharian Neolithic culture and the growth of its population**". (emphasis that of author)

Dr. Jelenick an expert on the Rock art of the ancient Sahara reports that the inhabitants of the Fezzan were round-headed

Africans (Jelinek 1985,p.273). The cultural characteristics of the Fezzanese were analogous to C-Group culture items and the people of **Ta-Seti** . The C-Group people occupied the Sudan and Fezzan regions between 3700-1300 BC (Jelinek 1985).

During the Neolithic period the western Sahara had many rivers. Today what we call the Niger river was divided into two rivers in c.5000 B.C. One was called the Upper Niger and the other the Lower Niger. The Upper Niger rose in the mountains on the border of Sierra Leone and flowed northeastward into a closed basin in the Sahara; downstream the river there were many wide marshes and several large lakes. The Lower Niger rose in the Hoggar mountains of the Saharan zone. It was fed by streams from the Adrar massif. Winds from the Atlantic ocean took rains into North and West Africa, which supported much vegetation in Neolithic times.

In the Tichitt region of Mauritania, an area, which is now desert there was a river, now dried up which flowed into the Senegal river. Lake Chad was then much larger with a river from the Hoggar called the **Tafassasset** emptying in it. Rivers also flowed from the Moroccan Atlas mountains into the western Sahara.

It would appear that the people who most influenced the history of North and West Africa after 4000 B.C. originally lived in the Fezzan region of Libya. The archaeological evidence supports an early division of the Saharan culture into two groups (1) Eastern Sahara , which shows affinity to the middle Nile cultures, which I believe was made up of Egyptian and Niger-Congo speakers; and (2) Western Sahara, which was made up of the Manding, Elamite, Dravidian, Sumerian and Nilo-Saharan speakers (Winters 1985a).

There are similarities between Egyptian and Saharan motifs(Farid,1985). It was in the Sahara that we find the first evidence of agriculture, animal domestication and weaving.(Farid 1985, p.82) This highland region is the **Kemites** "Mountain of the Moons " region, the area from which the civilization and goods of **Kem**, originated.

The rock art of the Saharan Highlands support the Egyptian traditions that in ancient times they lived in the Mountains of the Moon. The Predynastic Egyptian mobiliar art and the Saharan rock art share many common themes including, characteristic boats (Farid 1985,p. 82), men with feathers on their head (Petrie 1921,pl. xvlll,fig.74; Raphael 1947, pl.xxiv, fig.10; Vandier 1952, p.285, fig. 192), false tail hanging from the waist (Vandier 1952, p.353;Farid 1985,p.83; Winkler 1938,I, pl.xxlll) and the phallic sheath (Vandier 1952, p.353; Winkler 1938,I , pl.xvlll,xx, xxlll).

Due to the appearance of aridity in the Mountains of the Moon the neo-Atlanteans migrated first into Nubia and thence into Egypt. The neo-Atlantean origin of the Egyptians explain the fact that the Kushites were known for maintaining the most ancient traditions of the Egyptians as proven when the XXVth Dynasty or Kushite Dynasty ruled ancient Egypt. Farid (1985, p.85) wrote that "To conclude, it seems that among predynastic foreign relations, the [neo-Atlantean] Saharians were the first to have significant contact with the Nile Valley, and **even formed a part of the predynastic population**". (emphasis author)

The ancestors of the Egyptians originally lived in Nubia. The Nubian origin of Egyptian civilization is supported by the discovery of artifacts by archaeologists from the Oriental Institute at Qustul. On a stone incense burner found at Qustul we find a palace facade, a crowned King sitting on a throne in a boat, with a royal standard placed before the King and hovering above him, the falcon god Horus. The white crown on this Qustul king was later worn by the rulers of Upper Egypt.

Many Egyptologists were shocked to learn in 1979, that the A-Group of Nubia at Qustul used Egyptian type writing two hundred years before the Egyptians.(Williams 1987) This fact had already been recognized much earlier by Anta Diop (1974) when he wrote that it was in Nubia "where we find the animals and plants represented in hieroglyphic writing".

The Qustul site was situated in a country called **Ta-Seti**. The name **Ta-Seti** means "Land of the Bow". **Ta-Seti** was the name given to Nubia and a southern nome of   Egypt.

The Qustul incense burner indicates that the unification of Nubia preceded that of Egypt. The **Ta-Seti** had a rich culture at Qustul. Qustul Cemetery L had tombs that equaled or exceeded **Kemite** tombs of the First Dynasty of Egypt. The A-Group people were called **Steu** 'bowmen'.

The **Steu** had the same funeral customs, pottery, musical instruments and related artifacts of the Egyptians. Williams (1987, p.173,182) believes that the Qustul Pharaohs are the Egyptian Rulers referred to as the Red Crown rulers in ancient Egyptian documents.

Dr. Williams (1987) gave six reasons why he believes that the **Steu** of Qustul founded **Kemite** civilization:

1. Direct progression of royal complex designs from

Qustul to Hierakonpolis to Abydos.

2. Egyptian objects in Naqada III a-b tombs

3. No royal tombs in Lower and Upper Egypt.

4. Pharoanic monuments that refer to conflict in Upper
Egypt.

5. Inscriptions of the ruler Pe-Hor, are older than
Iry-Hor of Abydos.

6. The ten rulers of Qustul, one at Hierakonpolis and
three at Abydos corresponds to the "historical"
kings of late Naqada period.

Around the time the **Steu** , were migrating into Egypt and
the southern Temehu people settled Nubia and Kush, the Tehenu
were settling North Africa and the western Sahara.

MANDING CULTURE

The Olmec spoke one of the Mande languages, closely related
to the Manding group. As among the ancient Manding of Dar
Tichitt in Mauritania and along the Niger river, the Olmecs were
mound builders. Ancient Mexican traditions say that some of
their ancestors came from, a country across the sea, led by
Amoxaque or Bookmen. The Mexican term **Amoxaque** , agrees with the
Malinke-Bambara term **A ma nkye** , 'he [who] is a teacher'.

The founders of Olmec civilization were probably one of the Tehenu tribes, namely the Manding people of West Africa who speak a Mande language. This view is supported by Wiener who was able to identify the Manding origin of the inscriptions on the Tuxtla statuette. He also noted that practically all the religious ideology of the Mexica and Mayan people was derived from the Manding people of West Africa.

The dominant group in the early history of North and West Africa were the **Temehu** or C-Group people. The Temehu kept small livestock. They worshipped the goddess Neith. This is the goddess **Nia** of the Manding speakers.

The northern and Southern Temehu had different cultural dress. The southern Temehu were called **Nehasi** by the Egyptians wore a single shoulder strap attached to a high waistband. The Nehasi are mentioned quite frequently in the Egyptian literature of the 12th through 18th Dynasties. During these periods they were often employed as soldiers in the Egyptian army.

The northern Temehu were called **Tehenu**. They wore a crossed shoulder strap. The Tehenu also wore the characteristic cloaks, and penis sheaths. The descendants of the Tehenu include the Manding speakers of West Africa and the Dravidian speakers of

South India. (Winters 1985a, Anselin 1983) The Tehenu also founded Minoan Crete.

The Tehenus were centered around Sais.(El Mosallamy 1984, p.53) Sais was the religious center of Neith and serpent worship. According to Plutarch, it was at Sais, that Solon, the lawgiver of Athens learned about Atlantis.

The Temehus or C-Group people began to settle Kush around 2200 BC. The kings of Kush had their capital at Kerma, in Dongola and a sedentary center on Sai Island. The same pottery found at Kerma is also present in Libya especially the Fezzan.

The C-Group founded the Kerma dynasty of Kush. Diop (1986, p.72) noted that the "earliest substratum of the Libyan population was a black population from the south Sahara". Kerma was first inhabited in the 4th millennium BC. (Bonnet 1986) By the 2nd millennium BC Kushites at Kerma were already worshippers of Amon/Amun and they used a distinctive black-and-red ware. (Bonnet 1986; Winters 1985b,1991) Amon, later became a major god of the Egyptians during the 18th Dynasty.

Egypt, after the **Steu** formed the basis of the Egyptian people, due to declining patterns of weather after 2800 BC, people moved out of Nubia. As Egypt because more powerful, they soon began to conquer the many of the Temehu living in the

Western desert and Nubia. The southern Tehemu at Kerma were early conquered by the Egyptians. The northern Temehu remained independent until 1200 B.C.

Beginning around the rise of the New Kingdom in Egypt the Egyptians began to slowly conquer the Tehenu in the north. Under Thutmose III, the Egyptians began to push the Tehenu out of Libya. In the inscriptions of Queen Hatshepsut , the Queen with pride claimed that " my western boundary is a s far away as the mountains of **Manu** [the sun-set]...my fame is among the sand-dwellers altogether....I brought the tribute of Tehenu, consisting of ivory and seven hundred tusks which were there, numerous panther skins..." (El Mosallamy 1984, p.57) By 1312 B.C., the Tehenu, were crushed as a power in the western desert by Seti I.

Here we see clearly the popularity of "panther skin" clothing among the Tehenu. This love of panther skins among the Tehenu in Africa, was converted into love of jaguar skins when the Tehenu founded the Olmec empire in Mexico.

This defeat of the neo-Atlanteans of Libya, by Seti 1, set off a series of migrations in Libya, which sent the ancestors of the Olmecs southward into Saharan Africa and west Africa. The chariot routes of the Saharan zone indicate that although Egypt had taken much of Libya, the neo-Atlanteans of the Sahara continued to trade with Atlantis.

As the Sahara became more arid many Atlanteans began to move to other regions of Africa . Some of these Atlanteans were Mande speaking people from the Fezzan region of modern Libya.

The Temehus are called the C-Group people by archaeologists (Jelinek, 1985; Quellec 1985). The central Fezzan was a center of C-Group settlement. Quellec 1985, p.373) discussed in detail the presence of C-Group culture traits in the Central Fezzan along with their cattle during the middle of the Third millennium BC. They early invented boats. In addition, as the area became more arid they domesticated small horses and the ass to pull carts and chariots across the Sahara.

The Saharans first used boats and later the chariot for transportation. Many western scholars have argued that the "chariot people" of the Sahara were displaced Mycenians, because of the way the horses were depicted in gallop (Winters 1981b,1983). But the style of the chariots and manner of the harness proves they were of native origin. It must be remembered that many people in the Aegean area had formerly lived in the Western Sahara (Winters 1983b).

Apart from human and animal figures appearing on Nubian rock art, the most dominant motif during this period is the reed boat. Boats of identical design were also made in Mesopotamia and the Indus Valley. The first use of the mast and sails on reed boats, along with cabins on the deck appear at **Ta-Seti**, a country situated in Nubia 5000 years ago. An analogous boat with a cabin has been found on Izapa stela no.67 .

In the riverine cultures of Atlantean Libya, each community had marine architects, ship builders and expert sailors. The presence of an elevated bow and stern on many boats depicted in the Saharan rock art and the peculiar "bowstring", astern and "fuse" for the rudder oar, indicate these ancient ships were used for navigation on the open seas. Reed or plank boats are still made by the Dravidians in India, and the Bozo of West Africa, who live near the Niger river. Commenting on the reed boats of Africa and African naval technology Thor Heyerdahl, wrote: "In Egypt this ancient African type of vessel has died out long ago, but here [around Lake Chad] , isolated in the heart of the continent [of Africa] it still survived".[vi]

The goddess of the Atlanteans in Libya was Athena. The goddess according to Greek traditions was born near Lake

Tritonis.[vii] The goddess Athena, was called Neith by the
Egyptians and Nia by the Manding and Eteocretans (real) Minoans.

The father of Athena or Neith was **Poseidon** or Potidan "he
who gives drink, the wooden mountain" or boat (i.e., a boat on
the ocean is like a mountain on the sea) . The trident, which
was held by, Poseidon became recognized as a symbol of political
authority, was adopted by all the succeeding Atlantean
civilizations as their symbol of royalty.

Egyptian Serekh

(Note the three lines under the bird is the
serekh.)

This is evident in the fact that the trident, is a
identical to the **serekh**   of the Egyptians. The **serekh**
was the Egyptian sign for kingship. A bird is often placed
directly on the top of the Egyptian **serekh**.

The trident or **serekh** was also a sign for royalty
among the Olmecs. This **serekh** is found in many of the
inscriptions written by the Olmecs and also their
monuments.

On the monuments the Olmec **serekh** sign is more
rounded than that of the Egyptian style **serekh**. This sign
is evident in the mask face from Chalcatzingo Relief 2,
and the relief from Chalchuapa; and monument no. 52 from
San Lorenzo, the celt from Arroyo Pesquero,Veracruz and the
Las Limas figure (see figures 3 and 4).

The Greco-Roman writers made it clear that the
Atlantean civilization in Libya began to decline as the
Sahara became a desert. Due to radical tectonic movements
a catastrophe occurred which blocked springs that fed Lake
Tritonis. The Roman scholar Diodorus, wrote that Lake
Tritonis "disappeared from sight in the course of an
earthquake when those parts of it which lay towards the
ocean were torn asunder". Ovid, another Roman writer said
that the Sahara or Libya, became a desert after Phaethon's

conflagration. Ovid, in Metamorphoses Book II, wrote that "Then also Libya became a desert for the heat dried up her moisture".

The advent of hyper aridity led to the collapse of the Atlantean political control in much of the Sahara. High population density, and the resultant need for a reliable food supply forced the neo-Atlanteans to migrate out of the Sahara into other parts of Africa, Asia and Europe.

This climatic shift probably refers to the 4th and 3rd millennia when the Sahara began to become more arid. This aridity set in motion a number of migrations that forced the Atlanteans and their subjects to seek out new areas for settlement.

Apart from human and animal figures appearing on Nubian rock art, the most dominant motif during this period is the reed boat. Boats of identical design were also made in Mesopotamia and the Indus Valley. The first use of the mast and sails on reed boats, along with cabins on the deck appear at **Ta-Seti,** a country situated in Nubia 5000 years ago. An analogous boat with a cabin has been found on Izapa stela no.67 .

In the riverine cultures of Atlantean Libya, each community had marine architects, ship builders and expert sailors. The presence of an elevated bow and stern on many boats depicted in the Saharan rock art and the peculiar "bowstring", astern and "fuse" for the rudder oar, indicate these ancient ships were used for navigation on the open seas. Reed or plank boats are still made by the Dravidians in India, and the Bozo of West Africa, who live near the Niger river. Commenting on the reed boats of Africa and African naval technology Thor Heyerdahl, wrote: "In Egypt this ancient African type of vessel has died out long ago, but here [around Lake Chad] , isolated in the heart of the continent [of Africa] it still survived".[viii]

The goddess of the Atlanteans in Libya was Athena. The goddess according to Greek traditions was born near Lake Tritonis.[ix] The goddess Athena, was called Neith by the Egyptians and Nia by the Manding and Eteocretans (real) Minoans.

The father of Athena or Neith was **Poseidon** or Potidan "he who gives drink, the wooden mountain" or boat (i.e., a boat on the ocean is like a mountain on the sea) . The trident, which was held by, Poseidon became recognized as a symbol of political authority, was adopted by all the succeeding Atlantean civilizations as their symbol of royalty.

This climatic shift probably refers to the 4th and 3rd millennia when the Sahara began to become more arid. This aridity set in motion a number of migrations that forced the Atlanteans and their subjects to seek out new areas for settlement. One of these ancient settlements was Mexico, where the Neo-Atlanteans founded the Olmec.

Did Atlantis disappear in 1300-1200 BC

Diodorus Siculus, noted that in Egypt "Some men would maintain that in early times, before the movement of the sun had yet been recognized, it was customary to reckon the year by the lunar cycle. Consequently, since the year consisted of thirty days, it was not impossible that some men lived 1200 years.(Spanuth 1979,p.22) This suggest that when the Egyptians claimed that Atlantis had been destroyed 9000 to 8000 years ago, they may have been referring to months instead of years.

Jurgen Spanuth, in Atlantis of the North, has suggested that the Egyptians in ancient times used the term months to denote a year. He wrote that "Now if the 9000 or 8000 'years' of the Atlantis story are converted into the moon-months of the Egyptian calendar-a year has 13 moons-then we arrive at the period between 1252 and 1175 B.C.". (Spanuth 1979, p.22) These dates are interesting because it was around 1200 B.C. ,the Olmecs are believed to have suddenly arrived in Mexico. If Spanuth (1979) is correct this would place the Olmecs in Mexico sometime after the destruction of Atlantis.

Conclusion

In conclusion , the ancestors of the Olmec people were probably neo-Atlantean Mande speaking Tehenu. They came to Mexico from North Africa and the southern Sahara.

Because of the origin of the Olmec people in the Saharan colonies of Atlantis ,they shared many cultural elements with the Egyptians and Nubians. These cultural elements have been discussed by Wiener (1922), Sertima (1976) and R.A. Jairazbhoy .

Due to the new fauna and flora found in Mexico, and the different environmental features the **Xiu** people found in the New World they "reinvented" their culture to reaffirm their neo-Atlantean origins, but retain the unique ecological conditions they found in Mexico. The discovery of wheeled toys in Meso-America dating back to the Olmec period illustrate that the Olmec or **Xiu** people knew of the wheel. But the wheel was not necessary for communication purposes in Mexico because most Olmec settlements could be reached safely by boat.

Chapter 2

ANCIENT MIGRATION STORIES OF MEXICO

Stelae no.5 from Izapa, is an important historical document from Mexico. This monument has interesting iconographic representations that prove some of the migration traditions handed down from generation to generation by the Mexicans. The Izapa style art is characterized by upright stone stelae found at the site of Izapa, situated near Tapachula, Chiapas.

Izapa is located on the Pacific coastal plain in an area known as Soconusco. This area in middle preclassic times was a center of Olmec civilization (Morley,Brainerd & Sharer 1983: 64-66).

The research of the New World Archaeological
Foundation indicate that this site has been continuously
occupied since 1500 B.C. Much of what we know about the art
from Izapa comes from the work of Virginia Smith' Izapa
Relief Carving (1984), Garth Norman's Izapa Sculpture and
Jacinto Quirarte's Izapan-Style Art . V. Garth Norman
(1976) of the New World Archaeological Foundation has
published many of the stone stalae and altars found at
Izapa and discussed much of their probable religious
significance. Most researchers including Norman believe
that the Izapans were "Olmecoid". Smith (1984) disagrees
with this hypothesis, but Michael D. Coe (1962: 99–
100,1965:773-774, 1968:121), Ignacio Bernal (1969:172)
support an Olmec origin for the Izapan style art. Quirarte
recognized obvious Olmec cultural traits in the Izapa
iconography.

The Stelae no.5 from Izapa records many glyphic
elements common to other preclassic artifacts including the
jaguar, falling water, mountain, bird, dragon tree, serpent
and fish motifs (Smith 1984:28-29). This stelae also
provides many elements that relate to Mexican and Maya
traditions as accurately analyzed by Norman (1976:165-236).
Some ideological factors not fully discussed in regards to

this stelae is its discussion of elements of the Olmec religion, and the migration traditions of the Mexicans.

The Maya were not the first to occupy the Yucatan and Gulf regions of Mexico. It is evident from Maya traditions and the artifacts recovered from many ancient Mexican sites that a different race lived in Maya land before the Mayan speakers settled this region.

The Pacific area was early colonized by Olmec people in middle preclassic times (Morley, Brainerd & Sharer 1984). The Olmec civilization was developed along the coast of the Gulf of Mexico in the states of Tabasco and Veracruz (Pouligny 1988:34). The linguistic evidence suggest that around 1200 B.C., a new linguistic group arrived in the Gulf region of Mexico.

M. Swadesh (1953) has presented evidence that at least 3200 years ago a non- Maya speaking group wedged itself between the Huastecs and the Maya. Soustelle (1984: 29) tells us that "We cannot help but think that the people that shattered the unity of the Proto-Mayas was also the people that brought Olmec civilization to the region".

Friar Diego de Landa, in **Yucatan before and After the Conquest**, wrote that "some old men of Yucatan say that they

heard from their ancestors that this country was peopled by
a certain race who came from the East, whom God delivered
by opening for them twelve roads through the sea". In the
Popol Vuh, the famous Mayan historian Ixtlixochtl, the
Olmecs came to Mexico in **"ships of barks"**(probably a
reference to papyrus boats or dug-out canoes used by the
Proto-Saharans) and landed in **Potonchan**,which they
commenced to populate. Mexican traditions claim that these
migrates from the east were led by Amoxaque or Bookmen.
The term Amoxaque, is similar to the Manding phrase **'a ma
n'kye'**:"he (is) a teacher". These Blacks are frequently
seen in Mayan writings as gods or merchants.

Traditions mentioned by Sahagun, record the
settlement of Mexico by a different race from the present
Amerindian population. Sahagun says that these "Eastern
settlers of Mexico landed at Panotha, on the Mexican Gulf.
Here they remained for a time until they moved south in
search of mountains. Other migration to Mexico stories are
mention in the Popol Vuh, the ancient religious and
historical text compiled by the Quiche Mayan Indians.

This new race may have come from Africa. Sertima
(1976), and Weiner (1922) believe that some of these
foreign people may have come from West Africa. Dr.

Wiercinski (1972) claims that the some of the Olmecs were
of African origin. He supports this claim with skeletal
evidence from several Olmec sites where he found skeletons
that were analogous to the West African type black.
Wiercinski discovered that 13.5 percent of the skeletons
from Tlatilco and 4.5 percent of the skeletons from Cerro
de las Mesas were Africoid (Wiercinski & Jairazbhoy 1975).

The Mexican oral traditions of the Maya are
supported by Stela 5, from Izapa. In Stela No. 5, we view
a group of men on a boat riding the waves of an Ocean. At
the right hand side of the boat we see a personage under a
ceremonial umbrella. This umbrella was a symbol of princely
status. Above his head is a jaguar glyph, which according
to Dr. Alexander von Wuthenau indicates that he was an
Olmec. This personage has an African hairdo and a writing
stylus in his left hand. This Olmec scribe proves that the
Olmec had writing, which was deciphered by Clyde Ahmad
Winters in 1978 (Winters 1979; Wuthenau 1981).

In the center of the boat we find a large tree. This
tree has seven branches and twelve roots. The seven
branches probably indicates the seven major clans that form
ed the Olmec nation. The twelve roots of the tree which
extend into the waves of the ocean from the boat, probably

signifies the "twelve roads through the sea" mentioned by
Friar Diego de Landa.

Friar Diego de Landa (1978:8,28) , in **Yucatan
Before and After the Conquest**, wrote that " a certain race
who came from the East, whom God delivered by opening for
them twelve roads through the sea". This tradition is most
interesting because it probably refers to the twelve
migrations of the Olmec people. This view is supported by
the stone reliefs from Izapa, Chiapas , Mexico published by
the New World Foundation. In Stela 5, from Izapa we see a
group of men on a boat riding the waves (Wuthenau 1980;
Smith 1984 ; Norman 1976) .

It is clear that Stela No.5, from Izapa not only
indicates the tree of life, it also confirms the tradition
recorded by Friar Diego de Landa that the Olmec people made
twelve migrations to the New World. This stela also
confirms the tradition recorded by the famous Mayan
historian Ixtlixochitl, that the Olmec came to Mexico in
"ships of barks " and landed at Pontochan, which they
commenced to populate.(Winters 1984: 16) These Blacks are
frequently depicted in the Mayan books/writings carrying
trade goods.

In the center of the boat on Stela No.5, we find a large tree. This tree has seven branches and twelve roots. The seven branches probably represent the seven major clans of the Olmec people. The twelve roots of the tree extending into the water from the boat probably signifies the "twelve roads through the sea", mentioned by Friar Diego Landa.

ILLUSTRATION No.6
STELA No.5 IZAPA

Stela No.5

The migration traditions and Stela No.5, probably relates to a segment of the Olmec, who landed in boats in Panotha or Pantla (the Huasteca) and moved along the coast as far as Guatemala. This would correspond to the non-Maya speaking group detected by Swadesh that separated the Maya and Huasteca speakers 2000 years ago. Bernardino de Sahagun (1946) a famous authority on Mexico also supports the extra-American origin of the Olmecs when he wrote that A" Eastern settlers of Mexico landed at Panotla on the Mexican Gulf. Here they remained for a time until they moved south in search of mountains". The reported route of the Panotha settlers recorded by Sahagun interestingly corresponds to the spread of the Olmecs in Meso-America, which extended from the Gulf of Mexico to Chalcatzingo, in the Mexican highlands along the Pacific coast.(Morley, Brainerd & Sharer 1983, p.52)

Apart from human and animal figures appearing on Nubian rock art, the most dominant motif during this period is the reed boat. Boats of identical design were also made in Mesopotamia and the Indus Valley. The first use of the mast and sails on reed boats, along with cabins on the deck appear at **Ta-Seti**, a country situated in Nubia 5000 years ago. An analogous boat with a cabin has been found on Izapa stela no.67 .

In the riverine cultures of Atlantean Libya, each community had marine architects, ship builders and expert sailors. The presence of an elevated bow and stern on many boats depicted in the Saharan rock art and the peculiar "bowstring", astern and "fuse" for the rudder oar, indicate these ancient ships were used for navigation on the open seas.

Boat building has been known in Africa for thousands of years. Reed boats, and reed boat illustrations throughout Middle Africa. For example, today reed boats are still constructed by the Mande speaking Bozo people and Dravidian speaking people in India.

The boat has played an important role in Africa since prehistoric times. As early as Nagada I (4000-3500 BC) Africans were depicting boats on their pottery (Robert Partridge, Transport in ancient Egypt,(The Rubicon Press,1996 ,p.16). The same style boats are found in the Sahara at Tin Tazarift (J. Ki-Zerbo, "Old Masters of the New Stone Age", The Unesco Courier (1979) p.32; J Ki-Zerbo, African Preclassic Art. In General History of Africa: methodology and African Prehistory, (Ed.) by J. Ki-Zerbo (pp.672,676),1981). Between 3500-3000BC we find evidence of sails on pottery from Nubia and Egypt (Partridge, 1996, p.16). This proves that the sail was already in use in Africa Over 2000 years before the Mande speaking Olmec people set sail to settle Mexico.

The Proto-Olmec people, who lived in the ancient Sahara, were called Kushites. They settled many parts of the ancient world using their reed boats. The Prophet Isaiah mentions the expertise of the Kushites when he noted in the Bible at Isaiah 18:12 that: " Country of the whirring wings beyond the rivers of Cush, who send ambassadors by sea, in papyrus ships over the waters".

This indicates that as late as the Meroitic Kushite empire papyrus boast were still being used by Africans. Because the early civilization builders in Mesopotamia, the Indus Valley, Africa, and China after 3500 BC, originated in the Sahara there existed great similarity between boats engraved on rocks in Mesopotamia, Indus Valley/ India and ancient boats in the Sahara and Nile Valley (see Hornell, (1920) Indian Boat Designs", Mem. As. Soc. Bengal, 7(3) p.192).

Walter Resch, noted that apart from human and animal figures appearing on the Nubian rock drawings, the most dominant motif is that of reed boats (W.F.E. Resch, (1967) Die Felsbilder Nubiens, Graz), many of these boats like the boats at Nagada II, had sails. Henri Lhote during his 1956 expedition to the Highland Tassili region of Algeria also found reed boat engravings (H. Lhote, (1957) A la decouverte des freques, Paris).

Boats with sails were still being used in throughout Africa in 1500BC. Queen Hatshepsut of Egypt, recorded in her temple at Deir el Bahri a Puntite ship, which had sails and 60 oars. This indicates that African ships were usually prepared for sailing the oceans through the power of the wind, and /or by sail.

Punt is believed to be ancient Somalia/Ethiopia. The people who presently live in Ethiopia call the Puntite empire, the Arwe empire.

Other examples of reed boats have been found in Mesopotamia and the Indus Valley. It is among the engraved Saharan boats that we see the first use of masts and sails, along with cabins on the decks of ships as early as 3100 BC. The presence of this highly developed boat technology among the Proto-Mande provided them with the ability to sail to America 2000 years before the Mande speaking Olmec people established themselves along the east of Mexico. As a result the ancient Proto-Saharans share the same name for boat:

Dravidian (Tamil) Kalan

Sumerian   Kalam

Mande   Kulu

Papyrus boats were capable of traveling thousands of miles over the open seas. Earastosthenes, chief librarian of the Egyptian papyrus library in Alexandria said that papyrus ships, with the same sails and riggings as on the Nile sailed as far as Ceylon and the mouth of the Ganges (Indus Valley) (T. Heyderdahl, Early Man and the Sea, N.Y., p.23.)

Reed or plank boats are still made by the Dravidians in India, and the Bozo of West Africa, who live near the Niger river. Commenting on the reed boats of Africa and African naval technology Thor Heyerdahl, wrote: "In Egypt this ancient African type of vessel has died out long ago, but here [around Lake Chad] , isolated in the heart of the continent [of Africa] it still survived".[x]

The "mother civilization" of ancient America is called the Olmec civilization. The Olmec civilization was founded by Mande speaking people who presently in West Africa. The Olmec civilization is characterized by giant heads of African kings.

During the Neolithic period the western Sahara had many rivers. Today what we call the Niger river was divided into two rivers in c.5000 B.C. One was called the Upper Niger and the other the Lower Niger. The Upper Niger rose

in the mountains on the border of Sierra Leone and flowed
northeastward into a closed basin in the Sahara; downstream
the river there were many wide marshes and several large
lakes. The Lower Niger rose in the Hoggar mountains of the
Saharan zone. It was fed by streams from the Adrar massif.
Winds from the Atlantic ocean took rains into North and
West Africa, which supported much vegetation in Neolithic
times.

In the Tichitt region of Mauritania, an area, which
is now desert there was a river, now dried up which flowed
into the Senegal river. Lake Chad was then much larger with
a river from the Hoggar called the **Tafassasset** emptying in
it. Rivers also flowed from the Moroccan Atlas mountains
into the western Sahara. It would appear that the people
who most influenced the history of North and West Africa
after 4000 B.C. originally lived in the Fezzan region of
Libya.

These Proto-Saharans came to Mexico in papyrus boats.
A stone stela from Izapa,Chiapas in southern Mexico show
the boats these Proto-Saharans used to sail to America. The
voyagers manning these boats probably sailed down
TAFASSASSET, to Lake Chad and thence down the Lower Niger
River, which emptied into the Atlantic. This provided the

Mande a river route from the Sahara to the coast . These rivers, long dried up, once emptied into the Atlantic. Once in the Atlantic Ocean to Mexico and Brazil, by the North Equatorial Current, which meets the Canaries Current off the Senegambian, coast.

There are oral traditions and documentary evidence, which support the early migration of the Mande people to Mexico, called the Olmecs by the Amerindians. The Olmecs probably called themselves Xi or Shi people.

Conclusion

The Olmec civilization lasted from 1500 to 100 B.C. These Olmecs spoke an aspect of the Manding language.

In summary, the rock art from the Sahara, across Mesopotamia, and India are identical. It indicates that during Proto-Saharan times each community (Mande >Proto-Olmec, Sumerian, Dravidian, etc.) had marine architects, shipbuilders and expert sailors. The presence of an elevated bow and stern and the peculiar "bowstring" astern and "fuse" for the rudder oar, indicate that the ships used by the Proto-Saharans, including the Mande were used for navigation in the open seas.

It appears that some of the Olmec that later settled
in Mexico may have come from Tichitt in southern Mauritania
or the Arawan. At Tichitt there was a fairly large
population of Mande speakers before desiccation forced
these Proto-Manding people to modify their economy or move
southward to better-watered country. This Tichitt valley is
also an area where the western line of rock engravings
depicting the horse-drawn vehicles of pre-cameline times
are located. The Proto-Manding established chariot routes
from Libya down to the Niger Valley. It is intersecting to
note that the Manding term for maize is **"Ka"**, this agrees
with the Mayan term for maize **Kan**.

The appearance of Proto-Saharans in Mexico 3800
years ago resulted from paleoclimate changes in West Africa
after 2000 B.P. This view is supported by climatic studies
of the Dar(Dhar) Tichitt region, which show increasing
trends towards desertification. The trend towards more
severe dry seasons made much of West Africa unsuitable for
permanent human settlement.(Holl 1985:88) Competition for
decreasing arable land probably stimulated African
migration to new lands across the Atlantic and West Africa.

Due to the preoccupation of the Proto-Mande with
rainmaking during this period of climate change, led to the

importance of the rain maker in African society, and the snake who gave man the secrets to harness nature. This hypothesis is supported by the fact that in the Manding and Olmec languages **sa** means both rain and snake. Commenting on the association of the snake and rain making in Proto-Mande culture Augustin Holl (1985:108) wrote that: "In this regard the development of a symbolic mediator of stress in the form of rainmaking and its correlated snake cult seem a reasonable possibility. The general distribution of these features in Africa is strongly correlated with the distribution of the climatic pattern of two contrasting seasons"[one long and dry the other short and wet]."

Once the Mande and other Saharan people moved into the Savanna and Forest zones they began to discontinue the building of papyrus boats; except among the Budumu along Lake Chad and the Bozo on the Niger River . Most West Africans began to build dugout canoes due to the gigantic trees found in many parts of the Savanna and Forest zone.

Mexican traditions recorded by Sahagun, claim that these foreign people landed in Mexico at Panotha, on the Mexican Gulf. He said they remained here for a time until they moved "south in search of mountains". This traditions corresponds to the expansion of the Olmecs from the Gulf of Mexico to Chalcatzingo, in the Mexican Highlands.

The Olmec empire was spread from Yucatan in the East, to Guerrero and the Pacific coast on the west, through Guatemala, Salvador and Costa Rica on the Southwest. Here the Olmecs continued to use the Proto-Saharan script, which was later adopted by the Maya civilization.

Chapter 3

Neo- Atlantis: The FERTILE AFRICAN CRESCENT homeland of the Dravidian, African, Sumerian and Elamite People

The civilization and culture of many African Nations originated in middle Africa, which was a colony of Atlantis, in what is now the Sahara 10,000 years ago.

The original inhabitants of the Atlantis colonies in the Sahara, where ancestors of the Dravidian, Elamite and Sumerian people. They formerly lived in the highland regions of the Fezzan and Hoggar until after 4000 BC. This ancient Neo-Atlantean homeland of the Dravidians, Egyptians, Sumerians, Niger-Kordofanian-Mande and Elamite speakers are called the Fertile African Crescent. (Anselin 1989,pp.16; Winters, 1981,1985b,1991). We call these people the Proto-Saharans. (Winters 1985b,1991) The generic term for this group is **Kushite**. This explains the analogy between the Black African, Sumerian, Elamite and Dravidian

languages . The Egyptians called these Proto-Saharans Ta-
Seti and Tehenu. Farid (1985,p.82) noted that "We can
notice that the beginning of the Neolithic stage in Egypt
on the edge of the Western Desert **corresponds** with the
**expansion of the Saharan Neolithic culture and the growth
of its population**". (emphasis that of author)

The Homeland of the Proto-Saharans was that part of Middle
Africa we call the Sahara. Although today the Saharan
region is presently arid, around 8000 years ago this area
was a center for civilization, situated in a Mediterranean
climate.

This area was the original home of the Black African,
Egyptian, Elamite, Dravidian, Sumerian and Manding people.

Here the Proto-Saharans began as a single linguistic
community, which shared cultural traits that were fashioned
in their Saharan homeland. The Egyptians referred to this
area as God's land, the home of the Gods.

The linguistic evidence furnishes an abundance of
material, which supports the hypothesis of a historical
connection between the Dravidians , Elamites, Sumerian and
Black African languages. A unified cultural group probably

spoke the hypothetical Proto-language of this group over a
continuous part of middle Africa.

The history of the Proto-Saharans begins in the Sahara,
some seven to eight thousand years ago. The Proto-Saharan
speakers remained in this area until the Sahara began to
change from a Mediterranean to an arid climate. It was
after the migration of the Proto-Saharan peoples into Asia
and Europe that they came in contact with the Altaic,
Uralic and Indo-European speakers.

Archaeological evidence indicates that there was unity
between the Proto-Saharan populations in middle Africa.
Since the climate was wetter several thousand years ago,
the major crops were ensete, rice, sorghum, millet, sesame,
barley and fonio. Between 6000-5000 B.C.,the Sahara was
parkland with a Mediterranean vegetation. This period is
called the AFRICAN AQALITHIC. It is called the African
Aqualithic because of the

abundant streams, and rivers that dotted middle Africa at
the time. Due to the wet environment the Proto-Saharans
communicated mainly by boat.

The original homeland of the Proto-Saharans was in the
Saharan zone. The Saharan zone is bounded on the north by

the Atlas mountains, the Atlantic Ocean in the West, the tropical rain forest in the south and the Red Sea in the East. It was here that the ancestors of the founders of the river valley civilizations developed their highly organized and technological societies.

Ethnically the Proto-Saharans were round-headed Mediterranean of the ancient variety commonly called Negroes. For purposes of this book we will call this group Africoid. Around 7000 B.C. Mediterranean of a fairly tall stature not devoid of Negroid characteristics appears in the Sahara at Capsa

(now Cafsa)(Desange 1981). These Mediterranean's are called Capsians. This group flourished in an area extending from the western borders of North Africa into the southern Sahara. They lived on hillocks or slopes near water. But some Capsians lived on plains, which featured lakes and marshes. Their way of life continued from the Neolithic era up to the time of the Garamante.

Ceramics spread from the central and eastern Sahara into North Africa. These ceramics were of Sudanese inspiration and date back to the seventh millennium B.C. This pottery was used from Ennedi to the Hoggar .The makers of this

pottery were probably from the Sudan. (Desanges 1981) The
Capsian pottery tradition also came from the Sudan, and
first appeared at the valley of Saoura, and later at Fort
Flatters. This type of pottery probably originated at
Elmenteita in Kenya. (Ki-Zerbo 1979)

Skeletons of the Mediterranean type have been found
throughout Middle Africa, Southwest Asia, Mesopotamia,
Indo-Pakistan, Central Asia and China. It is no secret that
the founders of ancient Egypt, Elam, Sumer and the Indus
Valley were all of the Mediterranean type. These
Mediterranean people called themselves: KUSHITES.

The Kushites are known in history as bowmen and great
sailors. These Kushites called Group-A by archaeologists
founded the earliest empire in the World, in Nubia. The
first recorded empire on earth was located at Qustul, Nubia
around 3300 B.C.. This is over a hundred years earlier than
the founding of the Egyptian Empire. As a result the term
designating royalty in Egyptian **nsw** < **n y swt** = "(the man)
who comes from the south".

This empire was called Ta-Seti, or the Land of the Bow. It
was clear that the government and writing usually
associated with Egypt was first invented in Nubia, and

later carried down the Nile into Egypt. The people of Ta-
Seti, were called **"Steu"** or "bowmen". The Egyptians called
the area around Kush Tata-Neter "God's land".

The Kushites took the name Kush to many regions they
settled in Asia. The most important Kushite colony was
ancient Elam, i.e., **hatam** (Khaltam). The capital city of
Elam, was called **Kussi** by the Elamites. In Akkadian,Elam
was called Giz-bam or "the land of the bow". The ancient
Chinese tribes called the Elamites:**Kashti**. Moreover, in the
Bible in Jeremiah (xlxx,35) we find "bow of Elam".

Black-and-Red Ware (BRW)

These Kushites used a common red-and-black ware that has
been found from the Sudan in Africa, across Southwest Asia
and the Indian subcontinent all the way into China. The
earliest examples of the black-and-red ware of the Proto-
Saharans date to the early Amratian period 4000-3500 BC.
(Hoffman 1979) It was after 3500 B.C., and especially 2500
B.C. ,that the Proto -Saharans began to deeply affect the
activities of the Eurasian peoples.

The Amratian period of Middle Africa is the focal point for
the spread of BRW. There is affinity between BRW found at
Anau, in Russian Turkestan, and similar pottery from

southeastern Europe. Dr. J.G. Andersson (1934) found a similarity between pottery fragments found at Anau, and fragments discovered at Yangshao sites in Henan and Gansu province.

Chapter 5

Neo Atlantean Culture in the Proto-Sahara

Linguistic and archaeological evidence can help us to reconstruct the Proto-Saharan economy and social organization. The economy was diversified and shifted from hunter-gatherer to herder and later food producing as a result of the rise of consistent seasonal rains in Middle Africa after 7000

B.C. This regular rain led to the development of the mixed agriculture-herding economy of the Proto-Saharans. The bioarchaeological remains from the Sahara indicates a mixed economy based on the herding of cattle and goats, and the cultivation of barley. Over time the shifting Saharan environment limited , rather than determined the Proto-Saharan sedentary types of food producing technology.

The earliest horizon of the Sahara during the Late Pleistocene pottery and baskets were probably used by hunter-gatherer groups to collect grain, as evidenced by the abundance of millstones on early Saharan sites. Due to the richness of the flora and fauna in the Sahara during this period ethnic groups in Middle Africa were semi-sedentary hunter -fisher-gatherers who engaged in the exploitation of their habitat. These people may have had a limited interest in the domestication of plants and animals. But it was not until the return of an arid climate to the Sahara between 12,000 -7000 B.C. that the Saharans were forced to domesticate cattle and goats to ensure a reliable source of food. It was probably during this African Aqualithic that Proto-Saharans probably began to seriously domesticate/collect plants to supplement their diets.

The Paleo-climate of Africa explains the south and eastern migration of Negroes from North Africa and the Sudan respectively, into West Africa. There were various climates in Africa. In the Sahelian zone there was a wet phase during the Holocene (7500-4400 B.C.), which led to the formation of large lakes and marshes in Mauritania, the Niger massifs and Chad.(Talbot 1980) In the Niger area, the west phase existed in the eight/seventh and fourth/third millennia B.C. (McIntosh and McIntosh 1986:417)

There were very few habitable areas in West Africa during
the Holocene wet phase. According to McIntosh and McIntosh
(1986) the only human occupation of the Sahara during the
humid phase was situated in the Saharan massifs along
wadis. By the 8th Millennia Saharan-Sudanese pottery was
used in the Air region. (Roset 1983) Ceramics of this style
have been found at sites in the Hoggar. (McIntosh and
McIntosh 1983b:230) Dotted wavy-line type pottery has also
been discovered in the Libyan Sahara.

The pastoral-sedentary tradition is a highly developed
specialization exploiting food resources of the Savanna and
herding cattle throughout Middle Africa over 500 years ago.
The bioarchaeological remains from the Sahara indicates a
mixed economy for the Proto-Saharans based on herding of
cattle goats and sheep, and the collection of sorghum,
millet, yam and rice along the marshes and lakes.

The view that food production preceded pastoralism in the
Proto-Saharan case--at this junction in archaeological
research--is untenable. It would seem more reasonable to
assume that a hunter-gatherer group which clearly
specialized in the hunting of animals (as evidenced by the
abundance of arrowheads) would have moved from hunter-
gathering to animal domestication, since they would be

keenly aware of the habits of game, and therefore make the shift to animal husbandry rapidly when climatic conditions in the Sahara made it impossible to collect grains.

The return of rains during the African Aqualithic probably led to renewed interest in plant collection and later domestication. It was probably during this period that various groups began to specialize either in a pastoral or mixed-pastoral food producing economy. The fact that both of these economies held the best benefit for a stable society, may have encouraged the diverse Saharan ethnic groups to form some sort of "federal " relationship, which encouraged trade and cooperation between the varying peoples practicing different economies.

The contemporary nomadic pastoralist tradition in the Sahara was first introduced as a sedentary pastoral adaptation around 7000 years ago. At this time the Sahara was a mosaic of lakes and marshes united by permanent streams. The vegetation was Mediterranean and grew abundantly in the Saharan highlands, in Hoggar and Tibesti.

In addition to cattle, the archaeologist have found that the Proto-Saharans had abundant pottery and grinding stones. This wavy line pottery was first discovered at Khartoum, and dates to 4000 B.C.

The Proto-Saharans possessed millet and domesticated cattle and goats by 6000 BP. They were also exploiting the greenstone, in the Sahara, by 3000 BC1.

Greenstone is similar to jade. It is called amazonite. Saharan people probably got the amazonite from the Central Sahara: Gilf Kebir and Tibesti. This amazonite was made into beads. According to Strabo and Pliny the greenstone was still being mined in their day by the Garamante. The Expedition of the University of Chicago, to Niger reported in 2005 that the greenstone was used to make ceremonial disks, axes and small points.

The collection of plants also provided a reliable source of food during the formative stages of Proto-Saharan society. The discovery of large amounts of pottery and heavy grinding stones during this period at many sites suggest the possibility that pastoralist were more sedentary at this time.

A comparative study of the languages spoken by the Proto-Saharans(PS) gives us a very clear indication of their

1 Harry Thurston, Secrets of the Sands, (New York: Arcadia Publishing,2003) p.113.

cultural traits. The Proto-term for the Proto-Saharan
culture trait will be PS plus an asterisk e.g.,*PS. For
example the Proto-Saharans had chiefs PS: *sar, and lived
in cities/town PS:*uru. In these cities and between the
several cities they built roads PS:*sila.

Language	CHIEF	WRITING	CITY	PLACE
DRAVIDIAN	CA,CIRA	CARRU	UR	TA
ELAMITE	SUNKI,SALU	TALU	UR(U)	DA,TA
SUMERIAN	SAR	SAR, RU	UR	
MANDING	SA	SEBE,SEWE	FURU	TA

The Proto-Saharans called people or humanity PS:*oku. The
mother of the family was called PS: *amma or *ma ; and the
father was called PS:*pa. The children both boys and girls
were referred to as PS:*de/di/du. They lived in houses
called PS:*lu/du.

Due to the abundance of water during the African Aqualithic
the Proto-Saharans used the suffix PS:*-ta, to indicate a
place of habitation. They also used boats called PS:*kalam.

LANGUAGE	COPPER	GOLD	STEEL
DRAVIDIAN	URUTTIRAN	KANI,KANAM,KANNE	ALAVU,URUKKU
SUMERIAN	URUDU	GUSH-KIN	
MANDING	KURA, KU	SAANI	TUUFA
ELAMITE			UFA
PROTO-SAHARAN	*URUT	*ANI	*UFA

PROTO-SAHARAN WRITING

The Proto-Saharans had writing. They either engraved their
syllabic script in rocks, or used a stylus to engrave wet
clay. This view is supported by the fact that the term for
writing often has the long -uu, attached to various initial
consonants usually /l/, /r/, or /d/. For example writing in
Sumerian is Ru and Shu, Elamite Talu, and in Dravidian
carru. These terms agree with the Manding term for excavate
or hollow out du/do, kulu, tura, etc. This shows that the
Proto-Saharan term for writing denoted the creation of
impressions on wet clay or hard rock. The Sumerian term for
carving was du.

The Proto-Saharan script was the model script for the ancient Mande script, Proto-Elamite, Indus Valley writing and Linear A. The Proto-Saharan writing was first used to write characters on pottery, to give the ceramics a talismanic quality. Thus we find Proto-Saharans characters on ancient Chinese, Egyptian, Linear A and the Indus Valley.(Winters 1985).

The Proto-Saharans used water for communication purposes. Due to the abundance of water during the African Aqualithic the leaders of the Proto-Saharans were men that could tame the waters by dams, or building boats and habitation mounds safe from the numerous floods. Over time the Proto-Saharans formed a confederation of city states called the FISH CONFEDERATION.

MAA CONFEDERATION

The Fish or MAA Confederation had many culture features in common. For example they traced their roots back to the Sahara, especially Libya and Nubia. The principle god for these Proto-Saharans was Amon or Amun. In the archaeological literature these people are called Ta-Seti (A-Group) and C-Group people of ancient Kush/Nubia. The ancient Libyans were called Temehu, by the Egyptians. These

Temehu people are called by archaeologists C-Group people. The C-Group people settled much of the Sudan. The cylindrical tomb common to this area was also frequently built by other Proto-Saharans in Asia.

The Temehu kept small live stock. In addition to worshiping Amon, this Libyan group of Proto-Saharans worshipped the goddess Neith. In Europe she was called Athena, to the Manding and Minoans she was known as Nia.

The members of the Maa Confederation include the Egyptian founders of the New Kingdom, Elamites, Dravidians, Manding and the Sumerians. The God Amon of the Egyptians was taken to Egypt during the New Kingdom. The generic term used by the Proto-Saharans to refer to themselves was KUSHITE.

BOAT TECHNOLOGY

During the Aqualithic period the Proto-Saharans maintained well developed trade links with the east African homelands by boats which could travel across Africa along the numerous streams and rivers which dotted the more watered Middle African environment 8000 years ago.

The so-called Egyptian and Mesopotamian style boats are depicted in the Sahara at Tin Tazarift. These boats used by the Egyptians, Sumerians and Elamites are nothing more than the boats used by the Proto-Saharans. These boats were also used by the descendants of the Proto-Saharans in Mesopotamia and India. To navigate these boats the Proto-Saharans used celestial navigation.

Boat building has been known in Africa for thousands of years. Reed boats and reed boat illustrations are found throughout Middle Africa. Apart from human and animal figures appearing in Nubian rock drawings the most dominant motif is the reed boat. Other examples of reed boats have been found in Mesopotamia and the Indus Valley, both areas of early Proto-Saharan settlement. The first use of the mast and sails on reed boats, along with cabins on the deck appear at Ta-Seti, in Nubia over 3000 years ago.

In the riverine cultures of the Proto-Saharans, each community had marine architects, ship builders and expert sailors. The presence of an elevated bow and stern on many boats depicted in the Saharan rock art and the peculiar "bowstring", astern and "fuse" for the rudder oar, indicate these ancient ships were used for navigation on the open seas. Reed or plank

boats are still made by the Dravidians in India, and the
Bozo of West Africa along the Niger river.

Plant Domestication

· The earliest Neolithic farmers cultivated barley. They used
a wavy line ceramic style of Middle Africa referred to as
the Saharan-Sudanese ware.

The Proto-Saharans, once engaged in intensive agriculture
began to build towns. Complex political organizations and
craft specialization followed as certain ethnic groups,
clans became more and more sedentary.

The Proto-Saharans practiced a form of intensive
agriculture characterized by use of the hoe, related water
storage and irrigation techniques, plus the application of
fertilizers (manure) to the land.

The ability of the Proto-Saharans to produce surplus food
led to an increase in population and changes in social
organization. Naturally population increases forced the
ancestors of the Proto-Saharans to spill over into more

marginal areas. This forced them to domesticate plants and animals to preserve traditional levels of food production that had resulted from plant collection.

In Nubia the people long practiced agriculture. In 17000 B.C the people at Tushka were cultivating barley. The farmers at Tushka were the Anu people who first took civilization to Egypt and Mesopotamia.

At Kadero, a Proto-Saharan site in the Sudan we find that by 3310 B.C.,sorghum and millet was being cultivated. In Northwest Africa rice was being cultivated by 3000 B.C.

Land of cultivation was called *ga(n), in Proto-Saharan. Barren land near water that was cultivatable was called PS:*de(n)/di(n). The mainstay plant collected by the Proto-Saharans was millet and or sorghum. They took

this crop with them to Asia. The Proto-Saharans called their grain *se. The word for cultivate was PS:*be. They used the hoe PS:* pari, to cultivate the land. In addition they had dogs PS: *ur-, to help them hunt and watch over their domesticated stock.

Animal Domestication

The Proto-Saharans had a mobile life style and cattle was the mainstay domesticate. Much of the evidence relating to this pastoral way of life comes from the discovery of cattle bones at excavated sites in the Sahara, and the rock drawings of cattle found at many of these sites.

Bones discovered at desert sites inhabited between 7000-2500 B.C., indicate that residents here not only farmed but herded sheep, goats and cattle, when the Sahara blossomed.

Animal domestication in much of the Saharan zone came in response to the decline in resources around lakes and river valleys after 5000 BC when the Sahara entered a dry phase. (McIntosh 1980) The Proto-Saharans probably domesticated sheep and goats initially, and supplemented these animals with cattle. (Camps 1974) The Proto-Saharans called the sheep *kari.

A major Proto-Saharan site was Tadrart Acacus (9500-8500 B.C.). Here the people were reliant on pastoralism by 4000 B.C. They herded goat/sheep.

LANGUAGE	SHEEP	DOG	CATTLE,	COW,	OX	HORSE
DRAVIDIAN	KURI,KORI	ORI	NAKU		PARI,	IYULI
SUMERIAN	ZAR,SAR	UR	GUD		PARU	'MULE'
MANDING	SARA	WURU	GUNGA,KONGO		BARI,	WOLO /WOLU
PROTO-SAHARAN	*SAR	*UR-	*(N)GU		*PAR-	

The horse was known to the Proto-Saharans. This view is supported by the archaeological evidence, which indicates the remains of a small stature horse in North Africa, and its presence in Egyptian hieroglyph. In the hieroglyph the large Egyptian horse was called sesem, while the small Egyptian horse was called nefer. The term nefer, is analogous to PS *par.

The horse was just as common to Upper Egypt as in Nubia. This is supported by the fact that in Thebes as early as the 18th Dynasty Thebans rode horses bareback. They could not have got the horse from the Hyksos,because this group of Asians never conquered Thebes. Moreover, the appearance of Egyptians on horseback on the paintings found in the tomb of Menena, and the horse and rider in painted wood, dating to the early 18th Dynasty testify to the

horsemanship of the Egyptians. In addition horses are
depicted in the rock art of Nubia.

During the Neolithic Subpluvial (ca. 7000-6000 B.C.),
farming and herding were practiced by the Proto-Saharans in
the green savannas of the Sahara. Migrating Proto-Saharans
probably remnants of the future Egyptians took domesticated
cattle into the Nile Valley.(Hoffman 1979:102) These
pastoral people moved from the South into the Nile Valley,
not from the Southwestern part of Asia into the Nile
Valley.

The early Proto-Saharans made adequate uses of local game
and plant life, and they established permanent and seasonal
settlements around well stocked fishing holes. The
wanderings of this hearty folk were dictated by the varying
climatic conditions found in Middle Africa.

Hoffman(1979:218) commenting on the role of the Proto-
Saharans in the founding of Egypt observed that," A
exploration of the Western Desert (also known as the Libyan
Desert, or more generally, the Sahara) proceeds at an ever
quickening pace, it is now apparent that the despised
foreigners of Egypt's desert frontiers comprised a major
areal tradition roughly comparable to those of Upper and

Lower Egypt. Paradoxically, it was this desert tradition and not those of the Nile Valley that contributed to pre-historic Egypt those critical innovations like farming, cattle pastoralism, and long-distance trade that led to groundwork for her precocious civilization".

Variations in the weather patterns of Middle Africa forced the people to move from one area to the other depending on the environmental conditions resulting from changes in the climate. The first major migration of the Proto-Saharans from the nuclear Southern Sahara region occurred around 5200 B.C., when they began to move from the central Sahara, into the southern Sahara, and northwest Africa, back into Nubia. Beginning around 4200 B.C. the Sahara began to dry up. Many migrates fled the increasing harsh environment to settle much of West Africa, and Nubia , Equatorial Africa, and much of the Niger Valley at this time was probably still a forest zone.

For much of the African Aqualithic the Nile Valley was a swampy area. After the end of the European glacial period there was a decrease in the rainfall of the Sahara. This made the Nile Valley an attractive area of settlement for many Proto-Saharans, because as the Sahara became more arid the Nile Valley changed from a swampy hostile environment to one quite pleasant and habitable.

Due the decreased habitability of the Sahara, and the settlement of many Proto-Saharan populations in the choice areas of Middle Africa, which were not covered with forest or swampy areas where sickness was rampant, after 3500 B.C. many Proto-Saharans began to migrate out of the Sahara into Europe, Asia, and after 2000 B.C. the Americas.

To settle new areas the Proto-Saharans used their ability as navigators to transport entire tribes from Africa to Asia and Europe. The vessels of the Proto-Saharans were similar to the Egyptian style boats, as indicated by the boat depicted in the Sahara at Tin Tazarift.

The advent of hyper aridity led to the collapse of the Saharan culture. High population density, and the resulting need for a reliable food supply forced the Proto-Saharans to migrate out of the Sahara into other parts of Africa, Asia and Europe. The first group to migrate out of the Proto-Sahara was the Elamites and Sumerians.

The Nile Valley was already settled by the Proto-Egyptians and the A-Group people of Ta-Seti, so the Proto-Sumerians migrated into Mesopotamia while the Elamites made their way to Iran. These groups arrived in these areas by sea. They commenced to settle in Mesopotamia many cities formerly

settled by the Anu people, who had fled these cities as a result of the great flood after 4000 B.C.

The linguistic evidenced shows that the Elamites were basically a mixed group speaking Dravidian and Manding languages. These Proto-Manding and Proto-Dravidian elements migrated across the Zagros Mountains into Central Asia and China after 3000 B.C. Remnants of these Kushites made their way into the Indus Valley.

The Dravidian people of South India are the result of possibly two migrations from Africa into the Indus Valley and India. The Proto-Dravidians were probably remnants of the Proto-Saharan herders who occupied the central and southern Sahara until 2400 B.C., when hyper aridity began to dry up lakes, and cattle herding was more difficult. (Winters 1985,1989,1990)

Up until 2500 B.C., most of the Proto-Manding that had not made the migration to Iran were living in the Western Desert and the southern Sahara. This is supported by the archaeological evidence that indicates that the Sahelian and Sudanic zones were uninhabited by herders before 2500

B.C.(McIntosh and McIntosh 1981) After 2400 BC remnants of the Manding lived in Libya and began to settle Crete. The other major Manding sites were at Karkarichinkat, which was occupied until 2000 B.C. By 1500 BC the Proto-Manding lived in the Tichitt region.

The cultural and ethnic affinities of the Proto-Saharans encouraged the development of well organized trade relations between these groups in Africa and Asia. From the 4th Millennium through the 3rd Millennium B.C. an extensive trade network connected the Kushites/Proto-Saharans from Egypt to

the Indus Valley, Iran and West Asia. Homer alluded to the Kushite Diaspora when he wrote: "A race divided, whom the sloping rays, the rising and the setting sun surveys".

Archaeologists have found vessels from IVBI workshop at Tepe Yahya, in West Asia that have a uniform shape and design. This style of vessel is distributed from Egypt to Soviet Uzbekistan and the Indus Valley. These intercultural style vessels show clear parallels between Egyptian, Iranian, Sumerian and the Indus valley civilization.

The discovery of Intercultural style vessels from Susa (in Iran),Sumerian, Egyptian and Indus Valley sites suggest a shared ideological identity among these people. In fact the appearance of shared iconographic symbols and beliefs within diverse areas suggest cultural and ethnic unity among the people practicing these cultures. The common naturalistic motifs shared by the major civilizations include, writing (symbols), combatant snakes, the scorpion, bull and etc. This evidence of cultural unity is explained by the origin of these people in the Proto-Sahara.

Giant Stone Heads

The Proto-Saharans also made many giant stone heads. These stone heads over 2000 years old have been found in Ivory Coast and Senegal. These giant stone heads were made of granite and laterite hard stone. These stone heads 3 feet high may have been the proto-type for the Olmec heads made by the Olmec people in Mexico.

Chapter 5

The Mande-Atlanteans

The founders of Olmec civilization were probably
one of the Neo-Atlantean Tehenu tribes, was the Manding

people of West Africa. These people a Mande language. The idea that the ancient Olmecs may have been Mande speakers is supported by Leo Wiener, in **Africa and the Discovery of America.** Dr. Wiener identified the Manding origin of the inscriptions on the Tuxtla statuette . In three volumes of Africa and the Discovery of America, Dr. Wiener of Harvard University noted that practically all the religious ideology of the Mexica and Mayan people was derived from the Manding people of West Africa.

The dominant group in the early history of North and West Africa were the **Temehu** or C-Group people. The Temehu kept small livestock. They worshipped the goddess Neith. This is the goddess **Nia** of the Manding speakers.

The Olmec spoke one of the Mande languages, closely related to the Manding group of speakers found today in West Africa. Like the ancient Manding of Dar Tichitt in Mauritania and along the Niger river, the Olmecs were mound builders. Ancient Mexican traditions say that some of their ancestors came from, a country across the sea, led by **Amoxaque** or Bookmen. The Mexican term **Amoxaque** , agrees with the Malinke-Bambara term **A ma nkye** , 'he [who] is a teacher'.

One of the major groups of languages spoken in Africa is the Mande group. The Mande languages are divided into two groups, the Northern and South-Eastern Mande. (Winters 198bc)

The Northern Mande played an important role in world history. The Northern Mande languages include the (1) **Soninke** dialect cluster: **Azer, Bozo, Soninke (Sarakole)**; and (2) the Manding cluster: **Malinke, Bambara, Dyula** and **Vai**. Elements of the Northern Mande founded many civilization, including the Minoan civilization of Crete (Winters 1983b), the Olmec civilization of Meso-America (Wuthenau 1980; Winters 1979, 1981c,1986), and the Xia civilization of China (Winters 1980,1983c,1985d,1988, 1990).

The Proto-Manding are well known for their **totem** of a dragon or lizard (Winters 1983, 1983c,1985d). In ancient America and China this dragon or lizard totem was retained as the emblem of their civilizations.

The Proto-Manding often referred to themselves as **Si**. In the Manding languages the term **Si**, means "black, race, descendant and family". The plural in Manding was usually formed with the suffix /-u/. The term Si-u would mean the 'Blacks'.

The Yucatec Maya, called the people who introduced them to writing the **Xiu people**. The /x/ in Spanish is pronounced as /sh/ in 'she'.

The Mayan term Xiu agrees with the ancient name for the Manding people: **Si**. The fact that the Olmec people introduced writing to the Maya suggest that the Olmec peopled called themselves **Xiu** (Shi-u) 'the Blacks'.

Recent archaeological research in Africa suggest that although agriculture played a role in the spread of some African linguistic groups such as the Bantu and Cushitic speakers, cattle domestication led to the spread of other African groups across enormous parts of West Africa. This hypothesis suits the evidence we have regarding the spread of the Proto-Mande from the Saharan highlands in the east, to the shores of the Atlantic ocean in the west. (Winters 1986b)

Archaeological research from North Africa clearly illustrate the movement of semi-sedentary cattle herders from the Magreb and Saharan sites into West Africa. This agropastoral sedentary economy resulted in a growth in populations great enough to make it possible for the Mande speakers to expand across much of Northwest and West Africa between 5000 and 3000 years before the present (BP).

Archaeological evidence has increased in relation to prehistoric Africa in the past ten years. Linguistic material will be used to compliment the macrobotanical remains and evidence of material culture uncovered during archaeological excavation, so we can see clearly the subsistence and settlement patterns of the Proto-Mande.

The Mande speakers are often associated with the Niger-Congo family /superset of languages. Wm. Welmers (1971) has postulated an original homeland for the Niger-Congo Superset in the general vicinity of the Upper Nile. Ehret and Posnansky (1982) has suggested that the Mande diverged from the Kwa around 5000-4000 B.C. Dr. Welmers (1971) has hypothesized that around 3000 B.C. the Mande languages separated into Northern and Southeastern branches.

The Niger-Congo speakers probably inhabited the plateau and mountain regions of the Sahara: **Air, Ennedi, Tibesti and Hoggar.** These highland areas eight thousand years ago formed the **"Saharan Fertile Crescent"**. The linguistic evidence suggest that the Nilo-Saharan, Chadic, Egyptian and other supersets and subsets of languages also lived in this highland paradise.

Greenberg (1970) believes that during the Neolithic the Niger-Congo speakers had domesticated ovicaprids (sheep/goats). Winters (1986b) has illustrated that the Niger-Congo people utilized selected plant food including millet and rice .

Much of this discussion of the Proto-Mande migrations will involve discussion of the Mandekan or Manding languages of the Mande group of languages. (Platiel 1978; Galtier 1980) Mann and Dalby (1987) give Mande a peripheral status in the Niger-Congo superset.

The Manding languages include the Malinke-Bambara subset of the Northwestern Mande subgroup of languages. The original Manding lived in the southern Saharan highlands (Winters 1986b). Now the Mande are dispersed from the Sahara to the Atlantic Ocean in the so-called fragmentation belt of Africa.

The Manding languages have a high frequency of disyllabic roots of the CVCV,CV and CVV kind. Monosyllabic roots of the CV kind often reflect the proto-form for many Manding words. (Winters 1986b)

The Manding languages are genetically related to the Dravidian and Sumerian languages. (Winters 1983a,1985,1989) It also has affinity to Japanese (Winters 1983b), Coptic , and Magyar (Winters 1987; Zoltan 1985). Recently Winters

(1988) has shown that the Manding languages may be the substratum language of Tocharian. In addition, Manding shares many topological features with Amerind languages, including SOV/SVO sentence pattern, monosyllabic roots and agglutination (Welmers 1970).

Controversy surrounds the classification of the Mande language family. Greenberg (1963) popularized the idea that the Mande subset was a member of the Niger-Congo Superset of African languages. The position of Mande in the Niger-Congo Superset has long been precarious and today it is given a peripheral status to the Niger-Congo Superset. (Bennett & Sterk 1977; Dalby 1988) Murkarovsky (1966) believes that the Mande group of languages do not belong in the Niger-Congo Superset, while Welmers (1971) has advanced the idea that Mande was the first group to break away from Niger-Congo.

The Mande languages are also closely related to Songhay (Mukarovsky 1976/77; Zima 1989), Nilo-Saharan (Boyd 1978; Creissels 1981; Bender 1981) and the Chadic group. Zima (1989) compared 25 Songhay and Mandekan terms from the cultural vocabulary to highlight the correspondence between these two language groups. Zima

(1989:110) made it clear that "the lexical affinities between the Songhay and Mande languages are evident".

Mukarovsky (1987) has presented hundreds of analogous Mande and Cushitic terms. Due to the similarities between the Mande and Cushitic language families. Mukarovsky (1987) would place Mande into the Afro-Asiatic Superset of languages.

The traditional view of the dispersal of the Proto-Mande would place their original home in the woodland savanna zone of West Africa, in the area of the Niger Basin. (Ehret and Posnansky 1982:242) Bimson (1980) has proposed that the Mande migration waves originated from the Inland Niger Delta around 2000 BC.

This is a most attractive theory but it does not conform with the archaeological data collected over the past decade in Africa, that illustrates that until the second millennium B.C. the Inland Niger Delta was sparsely populated.(McIntosh & McIntosh 1981 ,1986)

The original homeland of the **Proto-Mande** was probably the Saharan highlands. (Winters 1986b) The archaeological data suggest that the Proto-Mande migrated first north (westward), and then southward to their present centers of habitation. (Winters 1981b:81)

By the late stone age (LAS) black Africans were well established in the Sahara.(Winters 1985b) These blacks were members of the Saharo-Sudanese tradition. (Camps 1974) These blacks lived in the highlands. The early Fezzanese and Sudanese were sedentary pastoralist.

We call these blacks Proto-Saharans. (Winters 1985b) Most of the Proto-Saharans lived on hillocks or slopes near water. But some Paleo-Africans lived on the plains, which featured lakes and marshes. During much of the neolithic/epipaleolithic period the Sahara resembled the Mediterranean region in climate and ecology.

Ceramics spread from the Central and Eastern Sahara into North Africa. These ceramics were of Sudanese inspiration and date back to the 7th millennium B.C. This pottery was used from the Ennedi to Hoggar. The makers of this pottery were from the Sudan. (Andah 1981)

In the Sahelian zone there was a short wet phase during the Holocene (c. 7500-4400 B.C.), which led to the formation of large lakes and marshes in Mauritania, the Niger massifs and Chad. The Inland Niger Delta was unoccupied. In other parts of the Niger area the wet phase existed in the eight/seventh and fourth/third millennia B.C. (McIntosh & McIntosh 1986:417)

There were few habitable sites in West Africa during the Holocene wet phase. McIntosh and McIntosh (1986) have illustrated that the only human occupation of the Sahara during this period were the Saharan massifs along wadis. By the 8th millennium B.C.

Saharan-Sudanese pottery was used in the Air. (Roset 1983) Ceramics of this style have also been found at sites in the Hoggar (McIntosh & McIntosh 1983b:230). Dotted wavy-line pottery has also been discovered in the Libyan Sahara (Barich 1985).

According to Jelinek (1985:273) the inhabitants of the Fezzan were **round headed blacks** . The cultural characteristics of the Fezzanese were **analogous to C-Group** culture items and people of Nubia.(Quellec 1985; Jelinek 1985) The C-Group people occupied the Sudan and Fezzan regions between 3700-1300 B.C. (Close 1988)

These early Paleo-Africans of Libya were called the Temehu by the Egyptians.(Behrens 1984:30) Ethnically the

Temehu had the same physical features of black African people. (Quellec 1985; Jelinek 1985; Diop 1984:72)

These **C-Group** people used a common black-and-red ware. B.B. Lal (1963) of the Indian Expedition in the Campaign to Save the Monuments of Nubia proved that the Dravidian people probably originally lived in middle Africa before they settled South India. A common origin for black Africans and Dravidians would explain the analogous cultural and linguistic features of these two groups. (Anselin 1982; Winters 1980,1981,1981b,1985a, 1985c)

The Proto-Mande speakers in the Saharan highlands were probably one of the numerous C-Group tribes settled in this area. If we accept this hypothesis the C-Group people would represent a collection of ethnic groups that later became the Supersets we now find in the fragmentation belt, such as the Niger-Congo speakers Greenberg (1970) believes early domesticated ovicaprids. The origin of the Mande among the sedentary pastoral C-Group ethnic groups supports the linguistic data indicating an early Mande domestication of cattle.

In the Sahara pastoralism was the first form of food production. Augustin Holl (1989) a specialist on western

Africa believes that pastoralism was the first form of food production developed by post-paleolithic groups in the Sahara.

In the eastern Sahara it would appear that ovicaprid husbandry preceded cattle domestication because cattle were maladaptive to rocky lands. This is in sharp contrast to the western Sahara where cattle was the mainstay domesticate for sedentary pastoral economies.

Much of the evidence relating to this pastoral way of life comes from the discovery of cattle bones at excavated sites in the Sahara dated between 7000-2000 BC, and the rock drawings of cattle. (McIntosh &McIntosh 1981) In the western Sahara, sites such as Erg In-Sakane region, and the Taoudenni basin of northern Mali, attest to cattle husbandry between 6000 and 5000 BP. The ovicaprid husbandry on the other hand began in this area between 5000 to 3000 BP. Cattle pastoral people began to settle Dar Tichitt and Karkarichinkat between 5000 to 3500 BP.

The first domesticated goats came from North Africa. This was the screw horn goat common to Algeria, where it may have been deposited in Neolithic times. We certainly see goat/sheep domestication moving eastward: Tadrart

Acacus (Camps 1974), Tassili-n-Ajjer , Mali (McIntosh &
McIntosh 1988), Niger (Roset 1983) and the Sudan. Barker
(1989) has argued that sheep and goats increased in
importance over cattle because of their adaptation to
desiccation.

It would appear that all the Proto-Mande were familiar
with the cultivation of rice, yams and millet. There are
similarities in the Malinke-Bambara and Vai terms for plant
domesticates. This suggest that these groups early adopted
agriculture and made animal domestication secondary to the
cultivation of millet, rice and yams. The analogy for the
Malinke-Bambara and Dravidians terms for rice, millet and
yams suggest a very early date for the domestication of
these crops.

Most of the Soninke speakers , on the other hand,
appear to have remained primarily pastoralist for a much
longer time than the Malinke-Bambara. The Bozo specialized
in fishing and the Marka were rice farmers.

The hypothesis that the ancestral homeland of the
Proto-Mande was in the Saharan highlands best explains
their migration routes into the Niger Basin, northwest and
west Africa in general. (Winters 1986b.) This hypothetical

migratory route for the Mande is supported by the diffusion of Saharan pottery styles dating from 2000-500 B.C., from the southern Sahara to the Inland Niger Delta. (McIntosh & McIntosh 1979:246,1983)

The archaeological and linguistic evidence suggest that changes in the Mande subsistence economy resulted from a combination of factors including demographic stress and ecological change. It was ecological change, which led to the Proto-Mande domestication of goats/sheep and cattle.

The Mande cultural lexicon makes it clear that animal husbandry, and not agriculture played a dominant role in the expansion of the Proto-Mande. The deep internal divisions for names for cultivated crops reflect the limited role of agriculture in the Mande dispersals.

The linguistic evidence suggest that the Malinke-Bambara early adopted agriculture after they migrated westward from the Fezzan and Hoggar regions.(Winters 1986b) The Soninke and South Eastern Mande speakers , on the other hand remained primarily pastoralist. As a result they adopted the names of cultivated plants used by the Malinke-Bambara or of agriculturalists they met in their travels.

The traditional view of the separation of the Proto-Mande (PM) would place the original their homeland in the woodland savanna zone of West Africa in the area of the Niger Basin 4000 years ago.[2] Although this is a popular and attractive theory, the archaeological data suggest that the original homeland of the Mande was more than likely the Saharan highland areas, and the southern Sahara 8000 years ago.

The PM were probably part of the Saharan Sudanese Neolithic[3], users of the dotted wavy line ceramics.(Winters 1986c,1986b) By the advent of the Neolithic the PM speakers had domesticated cattle and goats. They also cultivated millet.(Winters 1986c)

Between 3500 and 3200 B.C., the PM speakers left their original Libyan and Nubian homeland to settle the Hoggar and Fezzan(Winters 1985,1986c). They apparently migrated around the same time and remained more or less a single linguistic community.

By 2500 B.C., the Proto-Northern Mande (PNM) began to separate into two major groups. The Proto-Soninke were

---

[2]. C. Ehret and M. Posnansky, The Archaeological and Linguistic Reconstruction of African History (Berkeley: University of California Press,1982), pp. 241-243.

[3]. D.P. McCall, "The cultural map and time profile of the Manding-speaking people". In Papers in Manding, (ed.) by D. Dalby (Bloomington: Indiana University Press,1971), p.38.

spread from the Northern part of the Hoggar massif down into Mauritania. The Soninke speaking population of farmers and cattle herders were in Dar Tichitt by 3850 B.C. By 1500 B.C., there was wide spread settlement of the Proto-Soninke speaking Mande in Tichitt.

The Proto-Manding speaking population lived south of the Soninke in the Hoggar and in the Fezzan. These people were mainly farmers and fishermen. They had cattle but this was secondary to their farming and fishing. The Manding were a riverine people who built their habitation sites near rivers and streams. The towns communicated with one another by boats. Another group of Manding speakers, the Proto-Vai, went westward with the Proto-Soninke and lived in Dar Tichitt. (Winters 1986c)

According to Winters (1986c) the Proto-Manding speaking people lived south of the Soninke in the Hoggar and Fezzan. The Malinke-Bambara speaking Manding were mainly farmers and fishermen. They had cattle but this was secondary to their farming and fishing. The Manding were a riverine people who built their habitation sites near rivers and streams. The towns communicated with one another by boats. Another group of Manding speakers, the Proto-Vai , went westward with the Proto-Soninke and occupied the Dar Tichitt area.

In Dar Tichitt between 1500 to 300 B.C., cattle and goats appear throughout the region. By 1000 B.C., walls were built around the towns for protection from nomadic raiding parties. By 800 B.C. these towns stretched over a hundred miles of now uninhabited desert. (Munson 1976)

The distribution of the towns in Dar Tichitt during this period suggests the formation of a state or empire. Given the fact that the walls of the towns disappeared later, indicates that the various Soninke communities probably had a civilian army which was called up in times of emergency and also a standing army to deter the nomads who threaten settled Mande speaking communities.

In Dar Tichitt by 600 to 300 B.C., these Mande speakers lived in smaller towns situated in heavily fortified natural rock formations, which suggest that the inhabitants of the towns during this period were building their homes in areas which were easy to defend and offered natural fortifications. By 300 B.C., these towns were no longer inhabited.

Some researchers believe that the inhabitants of the Dar Tichitt towns were the **troglodyte Ethiopians** who lived in holes and were hunted by the **Garamante**, according to Herodotus, and sold into slavery. The rock engravings of Mauritania were presumably made to show the lifestyle of the people who lived there. Munson (1976), Winters (1986), Holl (1985,1985b,1989) believe that Tichitt, was the forerunner of the Soninke **Empire of Ghana**, given the fact that the people in this area continue to speak a Soninke language.

The **Garamante** lived in the Fezzan in the fertile valley between the Ubari Erg and the Erg of Murzuq in oases spread from al-Abiod to Tin Abunda. The last capital of the Garamantes was situated at Jerma.

The **Garamantes** may have been of Manding origin (Winters, 1983,1983b,1986c). The name Garamante seems to indicate that this group of Libyans, were members of the Mande community. This name in Manding means "Mande/Mantes of the arid lands". This analogy is supported by the name of the Mande group which translates into **ma** 'mother' and **nde** 'child', i.e., "mother's child"; **Bambara** or **Banbara** ,which means "separated from the mother", i.e., they follow descent from the father's side.

According to Robert Graves (1980, p.33), the Garamantes left the Fezzan and settled the south bank of the Upper Niger after they were subdued by the Lemta Berbers in the 2nd century A.D.

The presence of Mande communities in Mauritania and the Fezzan would explain the chariot routes that transverse the desert and end at the Niger bend. These routes suggest communication and trade between the Mande groups in northwest Africa, the Fezzan and the Niger bend. But it would appear that by the mid-first millennium A.D., all the Manding had left the Fezzan except for the Garamante.

By 2000 B.C., the Proto-Manding probably began to migrate from the Hoggar into the Tilemsi Valley, as the Sahara began to decline due to aridity. (Winters 1986c,pp.91-92) This was over 800 years after groups of Manding along with Dravidian speaking migrants moved out of the Hoggar and Fezzan into northern Libya and thence Crete and Asia Minor. (Winters 1983b,1989) A segment of this group also moved eastward and made their way to Iran after 3000 B.C., and from there into the Indus Valley (Winters, 1989,1990).

In the Tilemsi Valley the major center of Manding occupation was the Karkarichinkat site. The settlers of the Karkarchinkat site were herder-fisher collectors of a Saharan material culture (McIntosh & McIntosh 1981, p.608). The Proto-Mande expanded throughout Africa via the ancient river system, which formerly extended from the Saharan highlands to the Atlantic coast.

At Karkarchinkat north, herding and plant domestication were heavily practiced. The Bozo may have migrated along with the Manding into the Tilemsi Valley and settled first in the fishing communities of south Karkarchinkat. [4]

Sites in the Sahara, especially the Western Fezzan, have yielded plentiful bones of domesticated cattle and small stock, along with pottery shards and farming tools. These people had dug many wells. The pottery is of the Aqualithic type, and is found mainly in the Tilemsi massif and the Fezzan.

As more and more of the Sahel became arid, the Mande-speaking people began to move into the Niger Bend area after 500 B.C. (McIntosh & McIntosh 1979, 1981; Winters 1986c) Before 500 B.C., the Niger Basin was probably inaccessible by boat and/or uninhabited because of the presence of diseases detrimental to cattle and humans until the last part of the 1st millennium B.C.(McIntosh & McIntosh 1983, pp.39-42)

The early artifacts from the Niger area support a Saharan origin for the Manding of the Niger Delta. The bowl

---

[4]. B. Wai Andah, "West Africa before the Seventh Century". In General History of Africa, (ed.) by G. Mokhtar (Berkeley: Heinemann,1981),Vol.2: pp.593-619.

designs from the Niger Delta dating to 250 B.C., are analogous to pottery styles from the southern Sahara dating to between 2000-500 B.C. (McIntosh & McIntosh 1979,p.246).

The early settlers of the Niger were Malinke-Bambara and Bozo speaking people. They lived atop mounds. These riverine communities were partly vegetarian. The people also ate some meat and fish. Between Segou and Timbuktu, the people grew rice.

The pre-Islamic Mande established numerous communities. They specialized as farmers, fishermen and especially cattle herders until the decline in the environment of the Sahel. They grew rice, millet, sorghum, cotton, groundnuts, cow peas, okra, sesame and shea nuts. Other Mande people were fishermen as evidence by the bone-harpoons and terracotta net-weights from Donna Fatoma Ke-Bozo and Segoubougou.

The Mande also built megaliths carved in the shape of a phalli and human heads. The major sites with megaliths are Tondidaro and Kouga. They made ornaments out of copper. The dead were buried in jar-coffins. Often entire families were buried in the same mound complex.

Today the Manding people are Muslims. There ancestral religion was considerably different from the religion worshipped by the Manding today.

The pre-Islamic religion of the Malinke-Bambara (Mande/Manding speaking people) has been excellently recorded by G. Diterlen and Dominique Zahn. G. Diterlen, explains that in the mythical age the first ancestors of the Malinke-Bambara were transformed into birds and felines. As a result, their existed two cults (gyow/jow) among the Manding: the nama (feline) cult and the kuno (bird) cult.

The Proto-Manding worshipped Amon or Amma. After they migrated out of the Proto-Sahara into the bush they began to make new totems including lions and toads. There were two principal ancient Manding gods during this period in addition to Amma: Bemba and Faro. Bemba was recognized as the creator god, he was invisible to mankind. Faro on the other hand, was seen as an intimate god, a god that was present among mankind.

Faro was recognized as being androgynous, the witness of creation, and thus he was the image of the world created by Bemba. The human manifestation of Faro, according to Zahn, were twins, because they represented the two fold nature of Faro.

The members of the Manding komow or gyow/jow (secret societies) worn different mask during their ceremonies. These mask combined elements of the totems related to the Manding mythical feline and bird ancestors that were recognized as founders of the komow, along with horns on the masks.

The leader of the Manding secret societies (gyow or komow) or cults was called Tigi (chief). Dominique Zahn has made it clear that the tigi, often served as the political and religious leader of the village. The Olmec called these secret societies gyo/jo, in their inscriptions.

The nama society is the initiatory society of the traditional Malinke -Bambara. G. Dieterlen maintains that the nama cult was concerned with relations between human beings. It seems to insure communal unity and the defeat of sorcery. The aim of nama was, teaching people about the cult and the disciplining of people (sorcerers, thieves, etc.) who commit anti-social acts.

A major god of the ancient Manding people was a serpent god. This god was often associated with rain making and secret mysteries.

Chapter 6

Olmec Civilization

The Olmecs are credited with the founding of
civilization in Mexico. Controversy surrounds the exact
date for the Olmec civilization. We believe that this
civilization lasted from 1200 to 100 B.C. Other scholars
believe that the Olmec civilization lasted up until A.D.
600. These Africans built beautiful plazas in front of
their temples where they placed carved huge heads 8 feet
high, painted black and weighing tons. The Olmec
civilization was developed along the Gulf of Mexico in the
states of Tabasco and Veracruz.

The Olmec called themselves Xiu (Shiu). We call these people Olmec. The term Olmec is derived from the word **olli** (rubber). Another name archaeologist use to denote this ancient civilization was Olman, which was given to the coastal area of the Gulf of Mexico, where the artifacts of this culture were found. The people living in this region were called Olmeca.

The Olmec civilization is typified by large stone heads. This stone heads are believed to have been depictions of Olmec dignitaries.

The Olmec influenced many of the later civilizations of Mexico. Olmec colonies were spread from Guerrero and the Pacific coast, on the west, and through Guatemala, Salvador and Costa Rica on the Southeast.

The Olmec were accomplished artists , engineers and scientists. The Olmec civilization was so highly developed that it influenced all the other civilizations of Mexico. Jacques Soustelle, called the Olmec the **Sumerian**s of the New World.

The Olmec civilization was a riverine civilization. The rivers of Meso-America served as the major means of communication for the Olmec cities and outlaying towns.

The Olmec practiced swidden (slash-and-burn) agriculture. They cultivated maize, squash, manioc and probably cocoa.

The art of the Olmecs is characterized by large stone monuments, especially the heads of African rulers found at La Venta and San Lorenzo.

The Olmec iconography includes the so-called 'baby face' sculptures of Olmec infants. These infants played an important role in Olmec society, which we will discuss in detail later.

Olmec art is divided into two groups, the monumental and the personal art. The monumental art includes the gigantic stone heads, stelas and bas-reliefs. The personal art includes human figurines, ceramics, small stone sculptures, masks and axes.

The four major Olmec centers in Mexico were LaVenta , Laguna de Los Cerros, San Lorenzo and Tres Zapotes. The most extensive Olmec site was La Venta, an island near the Gulf of Mexico.

The island of La Venta is situated on the Tonala river. At La Venta archeologists have discovered numerous stone artifacts. La Venta was probably settled by the Neo-Atlanteans , because it was more than likely uninhabited when the Olmec arrived in Mexico, and it would have provided an easy site to defend against any attacks from the people living on the mainland.

At La Venta the Xiu constructed an elaborate complex of pyramids and large sculptured monuments weighting tons. Here the Olmec's efficient agricultural practices supplied them with an abundant food supply, which was used to support their large and highly developed society.

The Maya oral traditions support a extra Mexican origin for the Olmecs. Friar Diego de Landa , in Yucatan before and after the conquest , wrote that "some old men of Yucatan say that they have heard for their ancestors that this country was peopled by a certain race who came from the East, whom God delivered by opening for them twelve roads through the sea" (p.8) . This settlement is also alluded to in the Mayan epic the Popol Vuh.

Sahagun said that the Eastern people landed at Panotha on the Mexican Gulf, and went inland in search of mountains. The route mentioned by Sahagun corresponds to the trade routes of the Olmec, which led from the Gulf of Mexico, into the Mountains of Central America and Mexico. The three major Olmec trade routes were 1) a passage from central Mexico to Central America; 2) the southern route along the Pacific coastal plain; and 3) the northern route following the Yucatan coast.

San Lorenzo was another major center of the Olmecs. San Lorenzo was situated on the
Shores of the Coatzacoalca river south of the state of Vera Cruz.

Many stone monuments have been found at San Lorenzo. The mutilation of monuments at San Lorenzo, suggest that there was a revolt here, or it was invaded by non Olmec who destroyed the center.

The heartland of the Olmec civilization covers approximately 18000 sq. kilometers from El Viejon in the north, to La Venta in the southeast. This area was located in a vast tropical environment of lush tropical plain, traversed by the Pappaloapan, Coatzacoalcos and Tonala rivers, and their tributaries.

The discoverer of the Olmec of Mexico was Jose Maria Melgar of Seraro, who while visiting San Andres Tuxtla, of the state of Veracruz, found an enormous monolith sculpted in the form of a human head. He wrote that "as a work of art it is without exaggeration, a magnificent sculpture...but what most amazed me was that the type that it represents is Ethiopian. I concluded that there had doubtless been blacks in this region, and from the very earliest ages of the world". (Soustelle, 1984)

The first archaeologist to scientifically examine the remains of the Olmecs was Dr. Matthew Stirling (1939). When

Dr. Stirling discovered the giant sculptured heads that characterize the Olmec civilization, he noted that the head is "unique in character among aboriginal American sculptures, it is remarkable for its realistic treatment. The features are bold and amazingly Negroid in character".

Although Dr. Stirling, when he first discovered the Olmec heads at La Venta, and Mr. Melgar felt that Africans had early colonized Mexico, most if not all contemporary Meso-American archaeologist refuse to seriously regard the colossal Olmec heads as representing Africans. Although the Africoid somatic traits of the Olmec colossal heads astonish most archaeologists, these Eurocentric scholars maintained that Africans did not arrive in America until the Atlantic slave trade.

But Sertima (1976) Winters (1980,1981) and Dr. Wuthenau (1980) have presented considerable evidence supporting the view that many of the Olmecs were Africans. For example, the so called epicanthic fold (or Mongoloid eye) common to Olmec sculptures is also associated with the West African type of humanity, as is the full cheek, slanted eyes, thick lips and short broad nose--all of these characteristics are common to Olmec works of art.

SKELETAL EVIDENCE

Due to the tropical environment of the Olmec heartland, the "Hot Lands", the name given the are by the Amerindians few skeletal remains of the Olmecs have been found. Yet it is interesting to note that among those skeletal remains discovered in this area some appear to have African traits.(Wiercinski and Jairazbhoy,1975) In 1974, at the 41st Congress of Americanist in Mexico, Andrzej Wiercinski, a Polish craniologist commented on the presence of African Negroid skulls at the Olmec sites of Tlatilco, Cerro de los Mesas and Monte Alban. (Wuthenau 1980; Rensberger 1981) Dr. Wiercinski observed that these skulls show "a clear prevalence of the total Negro pattern that has been evidenced by the use of two methods: a) multivariate distance analysis of average characteristics of individual fractions distinguished cranioscopically; and b) an analysis of frequency distributions of mean Index of the position between combination of racial varieties. (Wuthenau 1980)

Dr. Wiercinski (1975) made it clear that the skulls relating to the Olmec strata are of the West African type. Dr. Wiercinski (1975) classified 13.5 per cent of the skulls from an early Olmec cemetery as Africoid. (Rensberger 1981)

LINGUISTIC EVIDENCE OF AFRICAN INFLUENCE IN ANCIENT AMERICA

The most influential group in the rise of American civilization were the Manding speakers of West Africa. The Manding speaking people founded the first civilizations in much of West Africa 3500 years ago. They also founded the Olmec civilization in the New World and left numerous toponyms in Mexico and Panama. (Winters 1977, 1979,1981,1983,1986b)

Although Wiener (1922) and Sertima (1976) believe that the Manding only influenced the medieval Mexican empire, the decipherment of the Olmec scripts and a comparative analysis of the Olmec and Manding civilizations show correspondence. (Winters 1979,1980,1981) The most important finding of Wiener (1922) was the identification of Manding inscriptions on the Tuxtla statuette. Although Wiener (1922) was unaware of the great age of the Tuxtla statuette his correct identification of the African origin of the signs on the statuette helped us to decipher the Olmec script.

The linguistic evidence suggest that around 1200 B.C., when the Olmec arrived in the Gulf, region of Mexico a non-Maya speaking group wedged itself between the Huastecs and Maya. (Swadesh 1953) This linguistic evidence is supplemented by Amerindian traditions regarding the landing of colonist from across the Atlantic in Huasteca (we will discuss this tradition later).

The Manding speakers were early associated with navigation/sailing along the many ancient Rivers that dotted Africa in Neolithic times. (McCall 1971; McIntosh and McIntosh 1981) These people founded civilization in the Dar Tichitt valley between 1800-300 B.C, and other sites near the Niger River, which emptied into the Atlantic Ocean. (Winters 1986a)

The Olmecs spoke a Manding language. (Wuthenau 1980) This has been proven by the decipherment of the Olmec inscriptions. Due to the early spread of the Manding language during the Olmec period Manding is a substratum language of many Amerind.

language.

The Manding languages are a member of the Mande family of languages.(Platiel 1978; Galtier 1980) Mann and Dalby (1987), give Mande a peripheral status in the Niger-Congo superset.

As has been shown throughout this book the Manding settled many parts of the ancient world. The Olmec language has a high frequency of disyllabic roots of the CVCV,CV and CVV kind. Monosyllabic roots of the CV kind often reflect the proto-form for many Manding words.(Winters 1979)

As in most other Olmec languages, words formed through compounding CVCV and CV roots, e.g., (**gyi/ji** 'water') **da-ji** 'mouth-water, saliva', **ny -ji** 'eye-water:tear'. Manding has a well established affixial system, typified by the use of suffixes as useful morphemes expressing grammatical categories. Although tone is important in the Manding languages, it was least important in the Olmec group.

It is clear that contemporary Amerinds share few if any biological characteristics with Africans. Yet Greenberg (1987) has found many Amerind and African cognates.

In addition to cognates, there are numerous toponyms, which unite the New World and Africa. (Vamos-Toth Bator 1983; Duarte 1895) For example, the Olmec/Manding suffix of nationality or locality **-ka**, is represented in Mexico as **-ca**, e.g., Juxllahuaca, Oaxoca, Toluca and etc. In addition Dr.

Vamos-Toth (1983), has found over fifty identical toponyms in West Africa and Meso-America.

Skeletal Evidence of African Olmecs

Dr. Wiercinski (1972) claims that the some of the Olmecs were of African origin. He supports this claim with skeletal evidence from several Olmec sites where he found skeletons that were analogous to the West African type black. Wiercinski discovered that 13.5 percent of the skeletons from Tlatilco and 4.5 percent of the skeletons from Cerro de las Mesas were Africoid (Rensberger,1988; Wiercinski, 1972; Wiercinski & Jairazbhoy 1975).

Diehl and Coe (1995, 12) of Harvard University have made it clear that until a skeleton of an African is found on an Olmec site he will not accept the art evidence that the were Africans among the Olmecs. This is rather surprising because Constance Irwin and Dr. Wiercinski (1972) have both reported that skeletal remains of Africans have been found in Mexico. Constance Irwin, in <u>Fair Gods and Stone Faces</u>, says that anthropologist see "distinct signs of Negroid ancestry in many a New World skull...."

Dr. Wiercinski (1972) claims that some of the Olmecs were of African origin. He supports this claim with skeletal evidence from several Olmec sites where he found skeletons that were analogous to the West African type black. Many Olmec skulls show cranial deformations (Pailles, 1980), yet Wiercinski (1972b) was able to determine the ethnic origins of the Olmecs. Marquez (1956, 179-80) made it clear that a common trait of the African skulls found in Mexico include marked prognathousness ,prominent cheek bones are also mentioned. Fronto-occipital deformation among the Olmec is not surprising because cranial deformations was common among the Mande speaking people until fairly recently (Desplanges, 1906).

Many African skeletons have been found in Mexico. Carlo Marquez (1956, pp.179-180) claimed that these skeletons indicated marked pronathousness and prominent cheek bones.

Wiercinski found African skeletons at the Olmec sites of Monte Alban, Cerro de las Mesas and Tlatilco. Morley, Brainerd and Sharer (1989) said that Monte Alban was a colonial Olmec center (p.12).

Diehl and Coe (1996) admitted that the inspiration of Olmec Horizon A, common to San Lorenzo's initial phase has been found at Tlatilco. Moreover, the pottery from this site is engraved with Olmec signs.

According to Wiercinski (1972b) Africans represented more than 13.5 percent of the skeletal remains found at

Tlatilco and 4.5 percent of the Cerro remains (see Table
2). Wiercinski (1972b) studied a total of 125 crania from
Tlatilco and Cerro.

There were 38 males and 62 female crania in the study
from Tlatilco and 18 males and 7 females from Cerro.
Whereas 36 percent of the skeletal remains were of males,
64 percent were women (Wiercinski, 1972b).

To determine the racial heritage of the ancient
Olmecs, Dr. Wiercinski (1972b) used classic diagnostic
traits determined by craniometric and cranioscopic methods.
These measurements were then compared to a series of three
crania sets from Poland, Mongolia and Uganda to represent
the three racial categories of mankind.

In Table 1, we have the racial composition of the
Olmec skulls. The only European type recorded in this table
is the Alpine group, which represents only 1.9 percent of
the crania from Tlatilco.

Table 1.Olmec Races	Tlatilco		Cerro de Mesas	
Racial Type	Norm	Percent	Norm	Percent
Subpacific	20	38.5	7	63.6
Dongolan	10	19.2	---	----
Subainuid	7	13.5	3	27.3
Pacific	4	7.7	---	----
Armenoid	2	3.9	---	----
Armenoid-Bushman	2	3.9	1	9.1
Anatolian	2	3.9	---	---
Alpine	1	1.9	---	---
Ainuid	1	1.9	---	---
Ainuid-Arctic	1	1.9	---	---
Laponoid-Equatorial	1	1.9	---	---
Pacific-Equatorial	1	1.9	---	---
Totals (norm)	52		11	

The other alleged "white" crania from Wiercinski's
typology of Olmec crania, represent the Dongolan (19.2
percent), Armenoid (7.7 percent), Armenoid-Bushman (3.9

percent) and Anatolian (3.9 percent). The Dongolan,

Anatolian and Armenoid terms are euphemisms for the so-

called "Brown Race" "Dynastic Race", "Hamitic Race", and

etc., which racist Europeans claimed were the founders of

civilization in Africa.

Table 2:		
Racial Composition:	Tlatico	Cerro de las Mesas
Loponoid	21.2	31.8
Armenoid	18.3	4.5
Ainuid+Artic	10.6	13.6
Pacific	36.5	45.5
Equatorial+Bushman	13.5	4.5

Poe (1997), Keita (1993,1996), Carlson and Gerven

(1979)and MacGaffey (1970) have made it clear that these

people were Africans or Negroes with so-called 'Caucasian

features' resulting from genetic drift and microevolution

(Keita, 1996; Poe, 1997). This would mean that the racial

composition of 26.9 percent of the crania found at Tlatilco

and 9.1 percent of crania from Cerro de las Mesas were of

African origin.

In Table 2, we record the racial composition of the

Olmec according to the Wiercinski (1972b) study. The races

recorded in this table are based on the Polish Comparative-
Morphological School (PCMS). The PCMS terms are misleading.
As mentioned earlier the Dongolan , Armenoid, and
Equatorial groups refer to African people with varying
facial features, which are all Blacks. This is obvious when
we look at the iconographic and sculptural evidence used by
Wiercinski (1972b) to support his conclusions.

Wiercinski (1972b) compared the physiognomy of the
Olmecs to corresponding examples of Olmec sculptures and
bas-reliefs on the stelas. For example, Wiercinski (1972b,
p.160) makes it clear that the colossal Olmec heads
represent the Dongolan type. It is interesting to note
that the empirical frequencies of the Dongolan type at
Tlatilco is .231, this was more than twice as high as
Wiercinski's theoretical figure of .101, for the presence
of Dongolans at Tlatilco.

The other possible African type found at Tlatilco and
Cerro were the Laponoid group. The Laponoid group
represents the Austroloid-Melanesian type of (Negro)
Pacific Islander, not the Mongolian type. If we add
together the following percent of the Olmecs represented in
Table 2, by the Laponoid (21.2%), Equatorial (13.5), and
Armenoid (18.3) groups we can assume that at least 53
percent of the Olmecs at Tlatilco were Africans or Blacks.

Using the same figures recorded in Table 2 for Cerro, we observe that 40.8 percent of these Olmecs would have been classified as Black if they lived in contemporary America. Rossum (1996) has criticized the work of Wiercinski because he found that not only blacks, but whites were also present in ancient America. To support this view he (1) claims that Wiercinski was wrong because he found that Negro/Black people lived in Shang China, and 2) that he compared ancient skeletons to modern Old World people.

First, it was not surprising that Wiercinski found affinities between African and ancient Chinese populations, because everyone knows that many Negro/African /Oceanic skeletons (referred to as Loponoid by the Polish school) have been found in ancient China see: Kwang-chih Chang The Archaeology of ancient China (1976,1977, p.76,1987, pp.64,68). These Blacks were spread throughout Kwangsi, Kwantung, Szechwan, Yunnan and Pearl River delta.

Skeletons from Liu-Chiang and Dawenkou, early Neolithic sites found in China, were also Negro. Moreover, the Dawenkou skeletons show skull deformation and extraction of teeth customs, analogous to customs among Blacks in Polynesia and Africa.

Secondly, Rossum argues that Wiercinski was wrong about Blacks in ancient America because a comparison of

modern native American skeletal material and the ancient
Olmec skeletal material indicate no admixture. The study of
Vargas and Rossum are flawed. They are flawed because the
skeletal reference collection they used in their comparison
of Olmec skeletal remains and modern Amerindian populations
because the Mexicans have been mixing with African and
European populations since the 1500's. This has left many
components of these Old World people within and among
Mexican Amerindians.

The iconography of the classic Olmec and Mayan
civilization show no correspondence in facial features. But
many contemporary Maya and other Amerind groups show
African characteristics and DNA. Underhill, et al (1996)
found that the Mayan people have an African Y chromosome.
This would explain the "puffy" faces of contemporary
Amerinds, which are incongruent with the Mayan type
associated with classic Mayan sculptures and stelas.

Wiercinski on the other hand, compared his SRC to
an unmixed European and African sample. This comparison
avoided the use of skeletal material that is clearly mixed
with Africans and Europeans, in much the same way as the
Afro-American people he discussed in his essay who have
acquired "white" features since mixing with whites due to
the slave trade.

A. von Wuthenau (1980), and Wiercinski (1972b)
highlight the numerous art pieces depicting the African or
Black variety, which made up the Olmec people. This re-
analysis of the Olmec skeletal material from Tlatilco and
Cerro, which correctly identifies Armenoid, Dongolan and
Loponoid as euphemisms for "Negro" make it clear that a
substantial number of the Olmecs were Blacks support the
art evidence and writing which point to an African origin
for Olmec civilization.

In conclusion, the Olmec people were called Xi. They
did not speak a Mixe-Zoque language they spoke a Mande
language, which is the substratum language for many Mexican
languages.

The Olmec came from Saharan Africa 3200 years ago.
They came in boats, which are depicted in the Izapa Stela
no.5, in twelve migratory waves. These Proto-Olmecs
belonged to seven clans, which served as the base for the
Olmec people.

Physical anthropologist use many terms to refer to the
African type represented by Olmec skeletal remains
including Armenoid, Dongolan, Loponoid and Equatorial. The
evidence of African skeletons found at many Olmec sites,
and their trading partners from the Old World found by Dr.
Andrzej Wiercinski prove the cosmopolitan nature of Olmec

society. This skeletal evidence explains the discovery of many African tribes in Mexico and Central America when Columbus discovered the Americas (de Quatrefages, 1836).

The skeletal material from Tlatilco and Cerro de las Mesas and evidence that the Olmecs used an African writing to inscribe their monuments and artifacts, make it clear that Africans were a predominant part of the Olmec population. These Olmecs constructed complex pyramids and large sculptured monuments weighing tons. The Maya during the Pre-Classic period built pyramids over the Olmec pyramids to disguise the Olmec origin of these pyramids.

Chapter 7

The Olmec Writing

The major evidence for the African origin of the Olmecs comes from the writing of the Maya and Olmec people. As mentioned earlier most experts believe that the Mayan writing system came from the Olmecs (Soustelle, 1984). The evidence of African style writing among the Olmecs is evidence for Old World influence in Mexico.

The Olmecs have left numerous symbols or signs inscribed on pottery, statuettes, batons/scepters, stelas and bas-reliefs that have been recognized as writing (Soustelle, 1984; von Wuthenau, 1980; Winters, 1979). The view that the Olmecs were the first Americans to 1) invent a complex system of chronology, 2) a method of calculating time, and 3) a hieroglyphic script which was later adopted by Izapan and Mayan civilizations, is now accepted by practically all Meso-American specialist (Soustelle, 1984).

The Olmecs probably founded writing in the Mexico. Schele and Freide (1990) have discussed the Olmec influence over the Maya. This agreed with Brainerd and Sharer's, The

ancient Maya (1983, p.65) concept of colonial Olmec at
Mayan sites.

In 1979, I announced the decipherment of the Olmec
writing (Winters, 1979). It is generally accepted that the
decipherment of an unknown language/script requires 1)
bilingual texts and/or 2) knowledge of the cognate
language(s). It has long been felt by many Meso-Americanist
that the Olmec writing met none of these criteria because,
no one knew exactly what language was spoken by the Olmec
that appear suddenly at San Lorenzo and La Venta in
Veracruz, around 1200 B.C.

This was a false analogy. There has been for over 50
years evidence that the Olmec people probably wrote there
inscriptions in the Manding language and the Manding
writing from North Africa called Libyco-Berber, was used to
write the Olmec language

To decipher an unknown script it is unnecessary to
reconstruct the Proto-language of the authors of the target
script. In both the major decipherments of ancient scripts,
e.g., cuneiform and Egyptian, contemporary languages in
their synchronic states were used to gleam insight into the
reading of dead languages. No one can deny, that it was
Champolion's knowledge of Coptic that led to his successful
decipherment of Egyptian hieroglyphics.

The view that Africans originated writing in America is not new. Scholars early recognized the affinity between Amerindian scripts and the Mande script(s) (Winters, 1977, 1979).

By 1832, Rafinesque noted the similarities between the Mayan glyphs and the Libyco-Berber writing. And Leo Wiener (1922, v.3), was the first researcher to recognize the resemblances between the Manding writing and the symbols on the Tuxtla statuette. In addition, Harold Lawrence (1962) noted that the "petroglyphic" inscriptions found throughout much of the southern hemisphere compared identically with the writing system of the Manding.

Constantine Samuel Rafinesque (1832) published an important paper on the Mayan writing that helped in the decipherment of the Olmec Writing. Rafinesque is credited with the founding of the scientific study of American Indian languages (Belvyi,1997). Using the linguistic sciences Rafinesque was able to discover that the American Indian languages were related to many languages spoken in the Old World, especially African languages. David Drew (1999) commenting on the contribution of Rafinesque to Mayan linguistics and the decipherment of the Mayan writing noted that: Rafinesque realized that the glyphs in the Codex and the inscriptions from Palenque were the same written language. He worked out the basic notation used by the Maya to represent numbers, and not only distinguished the Maya form of glyphic writing from the less developed Aztec picture writing, but also suggested a direct connection between the ancient Maya writing system and contemporary Chontal and Tzeltal Mayan languages (p.78).

Rafinesque published his work in the Atlantic Journal and Friend of Knowledge . The seminal paper on the Mayan writing was published in 1832, in an article titled "Second Letter to Mr. Champollion, on the Graphic systems of America and the Glyphs of Otolum or Palenque, in Central America". In this paper he discussed the fact that when the Mayan glyphs were broken down into their constituent parts, they were analogous to the ancient Libyco-Berber writing (Belyi, 1997) . The Libyco-Berber writing can not be read in either Berber or Taurag, but it can be read using the Manding language .

This was an important article because it offered the possibility that the Mayan signs could be read by comparing them to the Libyco-Berber symbols (Rafineque, 1832). This was not a farfetched idea, because we know for a fact that the cuneiform writing was used to write four different languages: Sumerian, Hittite, Assyrian and Akkadian.

I was able to read the Libyco-Berber signs because they are analogous to the Mande signs recorded by Delafosse (1899). These Mande speakers, or **the Si people** , now centered in West Africa and the Sahelian region formerly lived in an area where Libyco-Berber inscriptions are found (Winters, 1983, 1986). Using the Manding languages I have been able to decipher the Libyco-Berber inscriptions (Winters, 1983).

The second clue to the Manding origin of the Olmec writing was provided by Leo Wiener in Africa and the Discovery of America (1922,v.3). Wiener presented evidence that the High Civilizations of Mexico (Maya and Aztecs) had acquired many of the cultural and religious traditions of the Malinke-Bambara (Manding people) of West Africa. In volume 3, of Africa and the Discovery of America, Wiener discussed the analogy between the glyphs on the Tuxtla statuette and the Manding glyphs engraved on rocks in Mandeland.

I was able to test the hypothesis of Rafinesque
and Wiener through a comparison of the signs inscribed on
the Tuxtla statuette and the La Venta celts (Winters,
1979). Using the should values from the Manding symbols, to
read the La Venta celts I was able to decipher both the
celts and other Olmec inscriptions. I translate the Olmec
signs using the Manding language (Bambara-Malinke)
(Delafosse, 1955).

The Mande people often refer to themselves as **Sye** or
Si 'black, race, family, etc.'. The **Si** people appear to

have been mentioned by the Maya (Tozzer, 1941). Tozzer
(1941) claimed that the Yucatec Maya said that the **Tutul
Xiu** (shiu), a group of foreigners from **zuiva**, in Nonoualoco
territory taught the Maya how to read and write. This term
Xiu agrees with the name **Si,** for the Manding people (also
it should be noted that in the Manding languages the plural
number is formed by the suffix **-u, -w**).

Progress in deciphering the Olmec writing has depended
largely on a knowledge of the Malinke-Bambara (Manding)
languages and the Vai writing system (Delafosse, 1899).
This language is monosyllabic. The terms in the Manding
languages explain the characteristics of the Olmec
civilization.

The Olmec inscriptions are primarily of three types 1)
talismanic inscriptions found on monuments, statuettes,
vessels, masks, and celts; 2) obituaries found on celts and
other burial artifacts; and 3) signs on scepters denoting
political authority.

The Olmec script has two forms or stages : 1) syllabic
and 2) hieroglyphic. The syllabic script was employed in
the Olmec writing found on the masks, celts, statuettes and
portable artifacts in general. The hieroglyphic script is
usually employed on bas-reliefs, stelas (i.e., Mojarra, and

tomb wall writing. The only exception to this rule for Olmec writing was the Tuxtla statuette.

Syllabic Writing

The famous inscribed celts of offering no.4 LaVenta, indicate both the plain (Fig. 1) and cursive syllabic Olmec scripts (Fig. 2). In the cursive form of the writing the individual syllabic signs are joined to one another, in the plain Olmec writing the signs stand alone. The cursive Olmec script probably evolved into Olmec hieroglyphics.

The inscriptions engraved on celts and batons are more rounded than the script used on masks, statuettes and bas-reliefs. The pottery writing on the Los Bocas and Tlatilco ware are also in a fine rounded style.

There are a number of inscribed Olmec celts. Olmec celts found were in many parts of Mexico, including the celt from Offering No.4 at La Venta , the inscribed jadeite celt from near El Sitio, and the Black Stone Serpent Scepter of Cardenas, Tabasco. These are all fine examples of Olmec writing. All the translations of Olmec artifacts are based on the Manding dictionary of Delafosse (1921).

The Offering No.4 is a fine example of Olmec art and writing. This offering includes a number of figurines and celts.

The third engraved celt at La Venta offering no.4, was engraved in the cursive Olmec script (Fig. 2). In the text of the cursive script we find Pè's obituary.

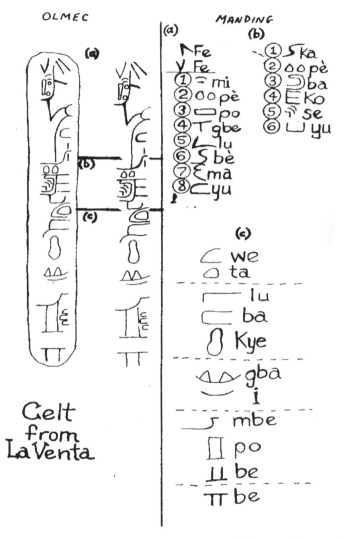

Transliteration of Symbols on Figure 1

Fè	fè	mi	pè	po	gbè
without breath	void	consumed	Pè	pure/holy	below (in)

lu	bè	ma
the family habitation	lay low the celebrity	(the) Lord (in)

yu	ka-pè	ba	ko
the big hemisphere tomb	Ka-Pè	the Great	(in) the back of

se	yu	we
(to) possess for posterity	the big hemisphere tomb	Hence

ta	lu	ba	i
this place	the family habitation	great/strong	thine

gba	kyè	be	po
fixed in the ground	inheritance/estate	here	pure/holy

mbe	be
lay low the celebrity	lay low the celebrity.

Translation

" Without breath. Void. Consumed (lies) the Hole Pè, below the family habitation. Lay low the celebrity, the Lord, in the hemisphere tomb. The Great Ka-Pè, in the back of the big hemisphere tomb, possesses (this place) for

posterity. Thine inheritance (is) fixed in this ground.
Here the pure celebrity lays low. Lay low the celebrity".

The fourth engraved celt from left to right in La
Venta offering no.4, is written in the plain Olmec script
(Fig. 1). This inscription declares that the tomb of Pè is
a talisman of great power.

Transliteration of Figure 1

Kyè	gyo			dè	gbè
A man	the leader of the cult			indeed	virtue
le	gyo	we	mbè	to	
to be	consecration	hence	here	place of rest	
he	gyo				
good	talisman.				

Translation

"The man (was) the leader of the cult. Indeed (a man of) virtue to be an object of consecration. Hence here a place of rest (a) good talisman (protective shrine for the faithful)".

Hieroglyphic Writing

There are two forms of Olmec hieroglyphic writing : the pure hieroglyphics (or picture signs); and the phonetic hieroglyphics, which are a combination of syllabic and logographic signs.

The characters written on the incised jadeite celt from El Sitio , Mexico was written in the hieroglyphic script .

This hieroglyphic writing represents compound syllabic Olmec characters in an ornate style, which probably evolved into the Mayan and Izapan hieroglyphic scripts. This ornate style of writing usually has two or more syllabic signs joined together .

El Sitio Figure

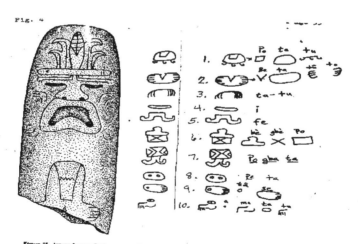

Fig. 4

Figure 25. Incised Jadeite Celt from near El Sitio Department of San Marcos, Guatemala At the right are the glyphs that are incised on the back of the celt. Height: 21 cm.

Transliteration of El Sitio Inscriptions

Po   ta   tu   bè   ta

Purity   here   take refuge   Bè   sacred
object/solitary

tu   to   ta   tu   i

Ruler   sequestered   here   place of rest
thou/you

fè   bè   gbè   po

in the company   unite   the pure   purity

po   gba   ta   pè   ta

purity   plant   propriety   to spread over this
place

se   ta   a   ta

to possess for posterity   sacred object   he   this place

ma   tu

ancestor/lord   rest.

Translation

"Purity, take refuge here. Bè is here. The Ruler is
sequestered (he who was righteous). Here is (his) place of
rest. You are in the company (of the Deity). Unite with the
purest of the Pure. Plant purity and propriety to spread

over this place (and) to possess for posterity. He (is) a
sacred object. This place the Lord rest".

In summary, the Olmec writing gives us keen insight
into the culture and civilization of the Olmecs. Knowledge
of this script can also help us learn more about the
ancient Olmec government and religion.

Chapter 8

Is the Olmec Writing African, Chinese or Mixe

The Olmec people introduced writing to the New
World. Many Meso-American accept the possibility that the
Olmecs were the first to 1) invent a complex system of
chronology; 2) a method of calculating time; and 3) a
hieroglyphic script, which was later, adopted by the Izapan
and Mayan civilizations (Soustelle, 1984). As a result, the
Olmec people left numerous inscriptions on monuments, celts
and portable artifacts that give us keen insight into the
Olmec culture, religion and politics.

The Olmec people introduced writing to the New World. Many
Meso-American accept the possibility that the Olmecs were
the first to 1) invent a complex system of chronology; 2) a
method of calculating time; and 3) a hieroglyphic script,
which was later, adopted by the Izapan and Mayan
civilizations (Soustelle, 1984). As a result, the Olmec
people left numerous inscriptions on monuments, celts and

portable artifacts that give us keen insight into the Olmec culture, religion and politics.

Over a decade ago Winters (1979, 1997) deciphered the Olmec writing and discovered that you could read the Olmec inscriptions using the sound value of the Vai signs. The Olmecs spoke and aspect of the Manding (Malinke-Bambara) language spoken in West Africa (Winters, 1979, 1980, 1981,1984).

Scholars have long recognized that the Olmecs engraved many symbols or signs on pottery, statuettes, batons/scepters, stelas and bas reliefs that have been recognized as a possible form of writing (Coe, 1965; Gay ,1973; Popenoe and Hatch , 1971 ; Soustelle, 1984). These experts recognized that the system of dots and bars whether associated with glyphs or not, found on Olmec artifacts probably indicated their possession of a system of chronology (Soustelle, 1984). As a result, we find that the Olmec monuments: Altar 7, of LaVenta; Stela no.7 of LaVenta; Monument E at Tres Zapotes; Stela C of Tres Zapotes; and the Tuxtla statuette are engraved with calendrical information (Morell, 1991; Soustelle, 1984).

Although many Meso-Americanists accept the view that the Olmecs possessed calendrical symbols controversy surrounds the presence of writing among the Olmecs. Wiener

(1922) and Lawrence (1961) have maintained that the Olmec

writing was identical to the Manding writing used in

Africa. Michael Coe and John Justeson on the other hand

believe that the Olmecs possessed a form of iconography but

not writing (Morell, 1991).

Over a decade ago Winters (1979, 1997) deciphered the

Olmec writing and discovered that you could read the Olmec

inscriptions using the sound value of the Vai signs. The

Olmecs spoke an aspect of the Manding (Malinke-Bambara)

language spoken in West Africa (Winters, 1979, 1980,

1981,1984).

Scholars have long recognized that the Olmecs

engraved many symbols or signs on pottery, statuettes,

batons/scepters, stelas and bas reliefs that have been

regarded as a possible form of writing (Coe, 1965; Gay

,1973; Popenoe and Hatch , 1971 ; Soustelle, 1984). These

experts accept the view that the system of dots and bars

whether associated with glyphs or not, found on Olmec

artifacts probably indicated their possession of a system

of chronology (Soustelle, 1984). As a result, we find that

the Olmec monuments: Altar 7, of LaVenta; Stela no.7 of

LaVenta; Monument E at Tres Zapotes; Stela C of Tres

Zapotes; and the Tuxtla statuette are engraved with calendrical information (Morell, 1991; Soustelle, 1984).

Although many Meso-Americanists accept the view that the Olmecs possessed calendrical symbols controversy surrounds the presence of writing among the Olmecs. Wiener (1922) and Lawrence (1961) have maintained that the Olmec writing was identical to the Manding writing used in Africa. Michael Coe and John Justeson (until recently), on the other hand believe that the Olmecs possessed a form of iconography but not writing (Morell, 1991).

The question is, can the Olmec decipherment claims made by some researchers be supported by the archaeological and linguistic evidence? The noted scholar Cyrus H. Gordon, in , claims that he has deciphered Linear A or Minoan, using the Semitic languages. Although he has made this claim, the decipherment is not accepted because it does not have collateral evidence to support the decipherment.

Maurice Pope in (1975), maintains that you reject a decipherment theory out right on three grounds: the decipherment is arbitrary, the decipherment is based on false principles, or the decipherment has been ousted by a better decipherment. The alleged Shang and Mixe-Zoque decipherments must be rejected because they are arbitrary and based on false principles.

Today there are three theories relating to the origin of the Olmec writing. The first theory is that the Olmec writing is an aspect of Malinke-Bambara. The other two theories maintain that the Olmec were Chinese speakers or speakers of a Mixe-Zoque language.

There are three problems with the Justenson and Kaufman decipherment of Epi-Olmec: 1) there is no clear evidence of Zoque speakers in Olmec areas 3200 years ago, 2) there is no such thing as a "pre-Proto-Soquean/Zoquean language, 3)there is an absence of a Zoque substratum in the Mayan languages.

First of all ,Justenson and Kaufman in their 1997 article claim that they read the Epi-Olmec inscriptions using "pre-Proto-Zoquean". This is impossible ,a "Pre-Proto" language Refers to the internal reconstruction of vowel patterns, not entire words. Linguists can reconstruct a pre-Proto language , but this language is only related to internal developments within the target language.

Secondly, Justenson and Kaufman base their claim of a Zoque origin for the Olmec language on the presence of a few Zoque speakers around mounts Tuxtla. Justeson and Kaufman maintain that the Olmec people spoke a Otomanguean language. The Otomanguean family includes Zapotec, Mixtec and Otomi to name a few. The hypothesis that the Olmec spoke an Otomanguean language is not supported by the contemporary spatial distribution of the languages spoken in the Tabasco/Veracruz area.

Thomas Lee in R.J. Sharer and D. C. Grove (Eds.), Regional Perspectives on the Olmecs, New York: Cambridge University Press (1989) noted that "...closely Mixe, Zoque and Popoluca languages are spoken in numerous villages in a mixed manner having little or no apparent semblance of linguistic or spatial unity. The general assumption made by the few investigators who have considered the situation, is that the modern linguistic pattern is a result of the disruption of an Old homogeneous language group by more powerful neighbors or invader." (p.223).

If this linguistic evidence is correct, many of the languages in the People who may have only recently settled

in speak Otomanguean family the Olmec heartland, and may
not reflect the people that invented the culture we
call Olmecs today.

Finally, the Justenson and Kaufman hypothesis is not
supported by the evidence for the origin of the Mayan term
for writing. The Mayan term for writing is not related to
Zoque.

Mayan tradition makes it clear that they got writing
from another Meso-American group. Landa noted that the
Yucatec Maya claimed that they got writing from a group of
foreigners called Tutul Xiu from Nonoulco (Tozzer,1941).
Xiu is not the name for the Zoque.

Brown has suggested that the Mayan term c'ib' diffused
from the Cholan and Yucatecan Maya to the other Mayan
speakers. This term is probably not derived from
Mixe-Zoque. If the Maya had got writing from the Mixe-
Zoque, the term for writing would probably be found in a
Mixe-Zoque language.

The fact that there is no evidence that 1)the Zoque
were in the ancient Olmec land 3200 years ago, 2)there is
no Zoque substrate language in Mayan, and 3) there is no
such thing as "pre-Proto-Zoque" falsifies Justenson and
Kaufman hypothesis.

Maurice Pope in <u>The story of Archaeological</u>
<u>Decipherment</u> (1975), maintains that you reject a
decipherment theory out right on three grounds: the
decipherment is arbitrary, the decipherment is based on
false principles, or the decipherment has been ousted by a
better decipherment. The Kaufman decipherment must be
rejected because it is arbitrary and based on false
principles.

The view that Africans originated writing in America
is not new. Scholars early recognized the affinity between
Amerindian scripts and the Manned script(s).

As noted in the previous chapter ,by 1832,
Rafinesque noted the similarities between the Mayan glyphs
and the Libyco-Berber writing. And Leo Wiener (1922, v.3),
was the first researcher to recognize the resemblance's
between the Manding writing and the symbols on the Tuxtla
statuette. In addition, Harold Lawrence (1962) noted that
the "petroglyphic" inscriptions found throughout much of
the southern hemisphere compared identically with the
writing system of the Manding.

The Olmec inscriptions are primarily of three types 1)
talismanic inscriptions found on monuments, statuettes,
vessels, masks, and celts; 2) obituaries found on celts and

other burial artifacts; and 3) signs on scepters denoting
political authority.

If this linguistic evidence is correct, many of the
languages spoken in this area are spoken by people who may
have only recently settled in the Olmec heartland, and may
not reflect the language of the people that invented the
culture we call Olmec today. This makes it very unlikely
that Mixe-Zoque was spoken on the Gulf 3200 years ago.

Mixe tradition also suggest that another people lived
in the Olmec heartland when they arrived in the area. In
The Mixe of Oaxaca: Religion, Ritual, and Healing, by Frank
J. Lipp it is noted that:

*"The elders say that there was a people who possessed
considerable knowledge and science and that they could make
children sick by simply looking at them. At one time they
came from a part of Veracruz and took up residence here.
However, they spoke a different language. Clearly, they
were also Mixe but their language was very modified, and we
did not understand the words they spoke"(p.77).*

Finally, the Justenson and Kaufman hypothesis is not
supported by the evidence for the origin of the Mayan term

for writing. The Mayan term for writing is not related to
Zoque.

Mayan tradition makes it clear that they got writing
from another Meso-American group. Landa noted that the
Yucatec Maya claimed that they got writing from a group of
foreigners called Tutul Xiu from Nonoulco (Tozzer, 1941).
Xiu is not the name for the Zoque. Brown has suggested that
the Mayan term c'ib' diffused from the Cholan and Yucatecan
Maya to the other Mayan speakers. This term is probably not
derived from Mixe-Zoque. If the Maya had got writing from
the Mixe-Zoque, the term for writing would Probably be
found in a Mixe-Zoque language. The fact that there is no
evidence that 1)the Zoque were in the ancient Olmec land
3200 years ago, 2)there is no Zoque substrate language in
Mayan, and 3) there is no such thing as "pre-Proto-Zoque"
falsifies Justenson and Kaufman hypothesis.

Michael Xu assistant professor of Chinese Studies at
Texas Christian University has proposed that the Olmec
people may have written in the Chinese language. He based
his opinion on the alleged similarity between the Olmec
writing and the Shang writing.

The Chinese wrote their inscriptions on Oracle bones.
These Oracle bone inscriptions were written by the Shang
people to divine the future.

152

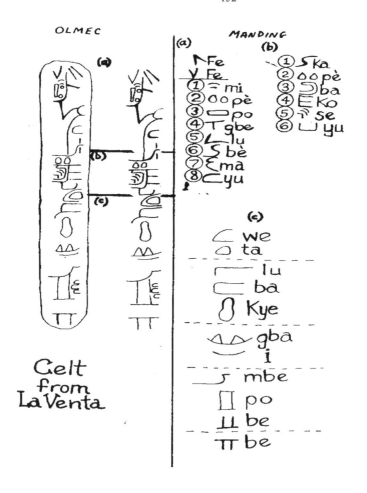

Celt from La Venta

This theory is fine except for the fact that the Olmec
writing has little affinity to the Shang writing. Moreover
some of the alleged similarities found by Xu do no relate
to Shang writing at all. Below is a table of Shang symbols.
A careful examination of the Shang table below and the

Oracle bone inscriptions above clearly show that none of these signs are identical to the Olmec writing found on the LaVenta celt.

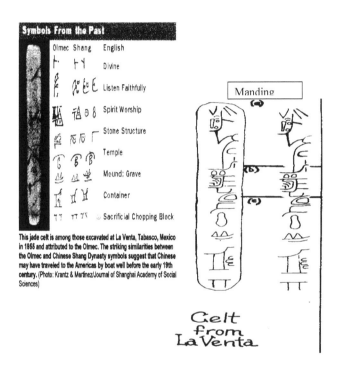

This jade celt is among those excavated at La Venta, Tabasco, Mexico in 1955 and attributed to the Olmec. The striking similarities between the Olmec and Chinese Shang Dynasty symbols suggest that Chinese may have traveled to the Americas by boat well before the early 19th century. (Photo: Krantz & Martinez/Journal of Shanghai Academy of Social Sciences)

Celt from LaVenta

A cursory examination of the Shang signs depicted in this table clearly show that they

do not match the alleged Shang signs identified by Xu in his article. In fact, a comparison of the actual signs on

the LaVenta celt and the alleged "Shang" signs lack any
agreement.

The view that Africans originated writing in America
is not new. Scholars early recognized the affinity between
Amerindian scripts and the Mande script(s).

By 1832, Rafinesque noted the similarities between
the Mayan glyphs and the Libyco-Berber writing. And Leo
Wiener (1922, v.3), was the first researcher to recognize
the resemblance's between the Manding writing and the
symbols on the Tuxtla statuette. In addition, Harold
Lawrence (1962) noted that the "petroglyphic" inscriptions
found throughout much of the southern hemisphere compared
identically with the writing system of the Manding.

The Olmec inscriptions are primarily of three types
1) talismanic inscriptions found on monuments, statuettes,
vessels, masks, and celts; 2) obituaries found on celts and
other burial artifacts; and 3) signs on scepters denoting
political authority.

Above is a celt discovered in the 1950's at La Venta
offering no. 4. This celt illustrates the similarities

between the Olmec and Mande/Vai writing systems. The famous inscribed celts of offering no.4 LaVenta, indicate both the plain and cursive syllabic Olmec scripts .

A comparison of the Olmec and Vai (Mande signs) above illustrate correspondence between the symbols. This affinity between Olmec and Mande signs supported the hypothesis of Wiener that the Tuxtla statuette was written in a Mande/Malinke-Bambara language.

The Olmec script has two forms or stages : 1) syllabic and 2) hieroglyphic. The syllabic script was employed in the Olmec writing found on the masks, celts, statuettes and portable artifacts in general. The hieroglyphic script is usually employed on bas-reliefs, stelas (i.e., Mojarra) and tomb wall writing. The only exception to this rule for Olmec writing was the Tuxtla statuette.

In the cursive form of the writing the individual syllabic signs are joined to one another, in the plain Olmec writing the signs stand-alone. The cursive Olmec script probably evolved into Olmec hieroglyphics. The inscriptions engraved on celts and batons are more rounded than the script used on masks, statuettes and bas-reliefs.

In conclusion the Olmec spoke a Mande language. They did not speak Chinese or Mixe-Zoquean. Recognition of Malinke-Bambara as the language spoken by the Olmec allow us to read the numerous Olmec inscriptions.

Chapter 9

Olmec Religion

The Olmecs had two different religious associations (gya-fa):the jaguar-man or humano-feline cult and the humano-bird cult. The humano-feline cult was called the nama-tigi by the Olmecs, while the humano-feline cult was called the kuno-tigi. The leader of the Olmec cult was called the tigi or amatigi "head of the faith". The tigi of the Olmec secret societies or cults exerted considerable influence both dead and alive. Alive he could contact the spirits of the deceased, and serve as intermediaries between the gods and mankind. Upon his death his grave became a talisman bestowing good to all who visited his tomb.

Dr. Sertima (1976) and Wiener (1922) have both commented on the possible relationship between the amanteca of ancient Mexico and the amantigi of Africa and the Olmecs. It is interesting to note that *tec / tecqui* means "master, chief" in a number of Mexican languages including Nahuatl (Wiener 1922).

Many Meso-Americanists have suggested that the Maya
inherited many aspects of their civilization from the Olmec
(Soustelle 1984). This is interesting because in the Maya
Book of Chumayel, the three main cult associations which
are suppose to have existed in ancient times were (1) the
stone (cutters) cult, (2) the jaguar cult and (3) the bird
cult. In lines 4-6 of the Book of Chumayel , we read that
"Those with their sign in the bird, those with their sign
in the stone, flat worked stone, those with their sign in
the Jaguar-three emblems-".(Brotherston 1979) The Book of
Chumayel, corresponds to the glyphs depicted on Monument 13
at La Venta .

On Monument 13, at La Venta a personage in profile, he has a headdress on his head and wears a breechcloth, jewels and sandals, along with four glyphs listed one above the other. The glyphs included the stone, the jaguar, and the bird emblems. Monument 13, at La Venta also has a fourth sign to the left of the personage a foot glyphs. This monument has been described as an altar or a low column.

The foot in Olmec is called "se", this symbols means to "lead or advance toward knowledge, or success". The "se" (foot) sign of the komow (cults) represent the beginning of the Olmec initiates pursuit of knowledge.

The meaning of Monument 13, reading from top to bottom, are a circle kulu/ kaba (the stone), nama (jaguar) and the kuno (bird). The interpretation of this column reading from left to right is "The advance toward success-- power--for the initiate is obedience to the stone cutters cult, jaguar cult and the bird cult". The Jaguar mask association dominated the Olmec Gulf region.

In the central and southern Olmec regions we find the bird mask association predominate as typified by the Xoc bas relief of Chiapas, and the Bas Relief No.2, of

Chalcatzingo. Another bird mask cult association was located in the state of Guerrero as evidenced by the humano-bird figure of the Stelae from San Miguel Amuco.

The iconographic representation of the Olmec priest-kings, found at Chalchapa, La Venta, Xoc and Chalcatzing indicate that usually the Olmec priest wore a wide belt and girdle. He was usually clean shaven, with an elongated bold head often topped by a round helmet or elaborate composite mask. During religious ceremonies the Olmec religious leader, depending on his cult would wear the sacred jaguar or sacred bird mask. Often as illustrated by the glyphs on the shoulders and knees of the babe-in-arms figurine of Las Limas element the mask would include a combination of the associated with the bird, jaguar and serpent.

The cult leaders of the bird mask cult usually wore claws on their feet. The jaguar cult leaders usually wore the jaguar mask.

Stelae No.5 also discusses in detail the two major Olmec religions: the nama (jaguar) komo (cult) and the kuno (bird) komo. At the top of Stela No.5 , we recognize two lines of Olmec writing across the top of the artifact. On the first line we read from right to left :I ba i. Lu tu

lu. I ba i, which means "Thou art powerful Now! Hold
Upright (those) obedient to the[ir] Order. Thou art
Powerful Now!" On the second line we read the following I
lu be. I lu , which means "Thou hold upright Unity. Thou
[it] upright"

The religious orders spoken of in this stela are
the Bird and Jaguar cults. These Olmec cults were Nama or
the Humano-Jaguar cult; and Kuno or Bird cult. The leader
of the Nama cult was called the Nama-tigi , or Amatigi

(head of the faith). The leader of the Kuno cult was the Kuno-tigi (Kuno chief see Illustration 6 Stela No.5). These cult leaders initiated the Olmec into the mysteries of the cult.

On the Stela No. 5, we see both the Kuno-tigi and Nama-tigi instruction youth in the mysteries of their respective cults. On Stela No.5, we see two priests and members of each cult society sitting in a boat with a tree in the center (Wuthenau 1980;Sitchin 1990,p.178). On the right hand side of the boat we see the Nama-tigi, and on the left hand side we see the Kuno-tigi.

Illustration No. 8
Kumo Tigi

Kuno Tigi

The personage on the right side of the boat under a ceremonial umbrella is the Nama-tigi . In Mexico, this umbrella was a symbol of princely status.

Above the head of the Nama Tigi is a jaguar glyph which, according to Dr. Alexander von Wuthenau (1980) indicates that he was an Olmec. This personage has an

African style hairdo and a writing stylus in his left hand. This indicates the knowledge of writing among the Olmecs which is also evident in the Olmec inscriptions deciphered by Winters (1977a,1977b,1979, 1980) .

On the sides of the boat we see two Olmec signs they read: "In the company of Purity". This statement signifies that the Olmec believed that worship of the Kuno or Nama cults led to spiritual purity among the believers.

Izapa Stela No.5

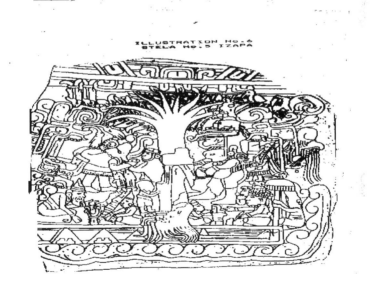

ILLUSTRATION NO.4
STELA No.5 IZAPA

On the left hand side of the boat we see a number of birds. Here we also find a priest wearing a conical hat instructing another youth, in the mysteries of the Kuno cult around a flame.

Among the Olmecs this flame signified the luminous character of knowledge. The Kuno priest wears a conical hat. The evidence of the conical hat on the Kuno priest is important evidence of the Manding in ancient America. The conical hat in Meso-America is associated with Amerindian priesthood and as a symbol of political and religious authority . Leo Wiener (1922, v.II) wrote that: "That the kingly and priestly cap of the Magi should have been preserved in America in the identical form, with the identical decoration, and should, besides, have kept the name current for it among the Mandingo [Malinke-Bambara/Manding] people , makes it impossible to admit any other solution than the one that the Mandingoes established the royal offices in Mexico" (p.3 21).

Meso-American archaeologists have been able to infer much concerning the Olmec civilization. These researchers have noted that the principal figure in Olmec art was a man-feline type resembling a jaguar.

The Olmec humano-jaguar cult was probably a carry over of the Neo-Atlantean ware-hyena cult of the Malinke-Bambara called **nama-tigi**. Among the Malinke-Bambara the hyena or **Nama** was recognized was recognized as the 'expert of the bush', due to his skill at survival in a harsh land. This honor was probably transferred to the jaguar when the Olmecs arrived in America.

In Africa, the hyena was the master of survival on the savanna. The jaguar probably both fascinated and terrified the Neo-Atlanteans when they arrived in Mexico. The fascination of the jaguar probably resulted from the jaguar's mastery of living in the torrid jungles of Meso-America. This made the jaguar the king of the jungle, and expert of the bush.

The jaguar probably came to represent the symbol for the Olmec government and leadership for two reasons. First, it was up to the Olmec priest-king to ensure the survival of the Xiu in the hostile jungles of Meso-America, This meant that the Olmec emperor and **tigiw** (chiefs) king had to be an *"expert of the bush"* like the jaguar to effectively lead their people.

Secondly, the jaguar, due to his behavior in the wild, signified man's awareness that he must control his passions and not be greedy if he was to live effectively and efficiently in the jungle. This is evident in the jaguar's habit of eating only enough food for his immediate survival.

This made the jaguar cult the major secret society in Meso-America. The jaguar was sculpted in jade and stone, often as a mask or in the form of the man-jaguar and the child jaguar. At Chalcatzingo, we find the female jaguar as well.

The mouths of the man-jaguar are usually toothless and indicate a child. This relates to the important role the Olmec placed on the cult associations as a method of socializing the children. The jaguar probably signifies man's awareness that he must control his passion and conforms to the rules of Olmec society. Consequently, the Xiu secret societies were used to train the human being in social relations.

The *tigi* or cult leader was recognized as experts in all aspects of life. But it appears that the cult specialists, specialized in the various branches of knowledge, i.e., medicine, masonry, agriculture and etc. The *tigiw* (chiefs) instructed the neophytes at special religious centers in the Olmec heartland.

Bernal believed that the Olmec centers at LaVenta, San Lorenzo, and elsewhere was dispersed cities. But the monuments left at these centers indicate that they were chiefly cult, and or ceremonial centers. Here youth were instructed in the Olmec cult beliefs and accepted social and religious behavior of the Olmec.

Many of the stelas found in the Olmec centers signify sites where cult association ceremonies were performed rather than "Long count" inscriptions. Eventhough the glyphs on these monuments appear to be dashes and dots similar to the Mayan numbers, some of these stela do not have accompanying glyphs indicating the period referred to by the "long count", such as the baktun and katun. Therefore the engraved Olmec stelas, except for Stela C, have little chronological data inscribed on them. These stelas were boundary stelas. Boundary stelas were stone monuments erected near a site with engraved characters describing the site as an Olmec cult center.

At Chiapas de Corzo, we have two interesting boundary stelas. They are Stela 6 and Stela 8. Below is a transcription of the most common signs on the boundary stelas.

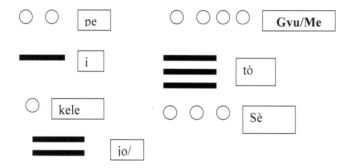

Below is the decipherment of the stelas from Chiapa de
Corzo, Stela 6 and Stela 8. At Chiapa de Corzo we read the
following, **Pe i kele tò se pe jo** ,"Vast (is) this area (it)
is unique (and) subject to the order. (Here learn the
skills) To make (one success(ful)).A vast (place)
consecrated to the divinity". In Stela 6, we read **Gyu i
kele sè jo de jo**, "The spirit on tranquility in the company
of a unique and vast talisman effective in providing one
with virtue. The *raison d'etre* this uncultivated land
consecrated to the cult". Stela 8, says **Gyu i gyu sè tò
kele tò sè i** , "Take root in the company of the spirit of

tranquility to realize obedience to the order (government).
It is a unique association to make a success of you".
Other stela were engraved with Olmec writing denoting the
outcome of initiation. Stelas in this category include
Monument E of Tres Zapotes and the Stela from Alvarado or
Cerro de la Piedra. The most common signs on these stelas
are ⌐_⌐ ba 'greatness, both physical and moral", and
ta ◯ 'place ,capture, area'.

Monument E of Tres Zapotes has three signs. This
monument is six feet tall.

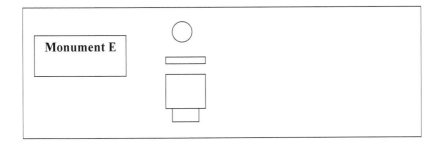

Reading Monument E, from top to bottom we have the
following **ta i ba** , 'Capture thou the Ba (Moral grandeur)'.

The stela from Alvarado is 12 feet 3 inches high. This
stela shows a standing personage in front of a bound
captive youth. The standing personage is handing the youth
the glyph po gbe 'pure righteousness".

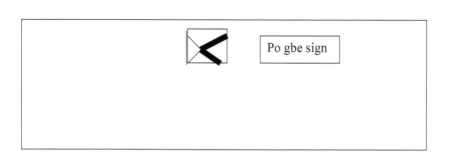

The bequeathal of *po gbe* to the bound Olmec youth adult dignitary appears

to represent the view that once a youth became a member of the cult

association s/he was bound to a righteous way of life forever.

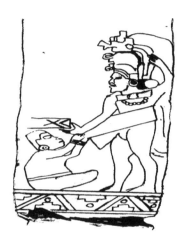

Alvarado Stela

Along the base of the Alvarado Stela we find two characters enclosed in a V. The

V can be interpreted as *fe* 'desire'. The other two signs are ***ta ba***. Together these signs

are *fe **ta ba***, and mean '(He) desires the capture of the Ba (moral grandeur).

    In the bush, the Olmec sculpted bas-reliefs, rather
than set up stelas to denote the location of an initiation
site. Two very good examples of bas reliefs used as cult

boundary signpost were carved at Chalchuapa, El Salvador.
Roberto Ibarra has published two very fine rubbings of
these carvings.

Fig. 24. Drawing and rubbings
by Roberto Ibarra of relief carving
from Chalchuapa, El Salvador

**Rubbings from Chalchuapa, El
Salvador**

These carvings provide us with the various clothing worn by the Olmec cult *tigiw* and associated glyphs. The Olmec signs are usually located in glyphs resting on the shoulder of the personages depicted on the reliefs.

This suggests that the bas-relief was meant to convey the fact that the priest in these bas-reliefs was the bearer of the laws of the religious association. In the Chalchupa rubbing No.1 we see three signs *fa,* *tò,* *la, fa tò la* , " abundant obedience to the law/cult (is) a good situation (for man)". There are two signs associated with figure No.2, *gbe,* *tò, gbe tò* , "Righteousness is obedience to the law/cult".

The Olmec Priest

The jaguar mask *komow* dominated the Olmec region. In the central and southern Olmec regions we find the bird mask komow predominates as typified by the Xoc bas-relief of Chiapas, and Bas-Relief No.2 of Chalcatzingo. Another bird mask *komo* was located in the State of Guerrero, as evidenced by the humano-bird figure of the stela from San Miguel Amuco.

The Olmec priest usually wore a wide belt and girdle. He was usually clean-, with an elongated bold head. During ceremonies the Olmec jo-fa "father of the cult association", depending on his komo, would wear the sacred jaguar mask or the sacred bird mask.

Often as illustrated by the glyphs on the shoulder and knees of the bebe-in-arms figure of Las Limas element , the mask might include a combination of bird and serpent elements.

The *tigiw* of the *kuno komo* usually wore a bird mask and claws on their feet. Although these aspects of the *kuno-tigi* regalia remain constant, the headdress worn by the *kuno-tigi* depending on his duties show considerable diversity.

In general, the humano-feline representation characterizes Olmec art. This humano-feline *jo-fa*, probably held both religious and political powers. The scepter was usually a symbol of the office of the *ba jo fa,* 'master cult association father'.

The man-felines usually have one glyph associated with this form of Olmec iconography. This sign is the St. Andrews cross inside a box   . This sign means *po-gbe* 'pure virtue' or 'Holy Purity/Virtue'.

The importance of the **jo-fa** in the Olmec komo is made evident in the glyph engraved eight times on the babe-in-arms stone figure from Las Limas. The Las Limas glyph has three signs in it **fa y(a) ta**, which means ' a father obedient to the order/cult association'.

The Xoc and Chalcatzingo bas-reliefs provide us with important information concerning Olmec cult association practices. The customs and headdresses of the personages on these reliefs inform us about their function and goals.

The Xoc bas-relief is found in the Valley of the Jalata river, a tributary of the Usumacinta, on the rim of the Lacandon Jungle. In addition to the bas-relief , the Xoc site includes several mounds and the remains of buildings.

The *jo fa* of Xoc is a carved on the flat limestone rockface. The *jo fa* is a short heavyset man wearing a loincloth supported by a wide girdle. He wears the bird mask and bird claws on his feet. A baton or scepter is held in his right hand, and an inscribed tablet is cradled in his left arm.

The headdress of the Xoc figure is elaborate and composed of many diverse symbols. It appears that the helmet or headdress/mask may be a compound of various Olmec characters. The symbols, which make up the Olmec masks and headdress capture the essence of the goals and capabilities of the cult association. These masks thus contain powers or energies from the words they incorporate in their construction that the wearers tap when they are worn.

A decipherment of these characters indicates that the duties of the Xoc priest were to increase the agricultural fertility of the land. The symbols on the Xoc figure's headdress are the following *ga* 'grow', *ka* 'maize, *su* ' stalk of a plant, habitation, *nde* 'uncultivated land' , and *po* 'pure,holy'. The headdress can be read as follows *ga ka su* 'Grow the maize plant(s)', *nde po* 'The uncultivated land is pure'. The phrase *nde po* can also be interpreted as follows, "The holy land near the point of inundation' and 'The pure grain',

Another symbol on the headdress, is the cross with circles on it. This sign means *gbe ta* 'To carry virtue' or 'Place of righteousness'.

The tablet carried by the Xoc *jo-fa* also has glyphs on it. The tablet is engraved with an image of a grown plant . This engraving is composed of two signs *gba ta*, which means "Act to plant (crops) this spot".

Relief No.2 Chalcatzingo

Chalcatzingo relief No.2, gives us considerable information on the **kuno komo**. In this relief we find several categories of the cult specialists both masked and unmasked.

On Chalcatzingo Relief No. 2, we find four figures. From left to right we a man with a typical Olmec face holding a leafy branch or a maize stalk in his hands in the far left corner. Next to him we find two personages carrying paddles. These figures on the Chalcatzingo relief combine the features of a bird with a long curved beak and the fangs of a feline. This *jo-faw* is carrying paddles or boards.

The fourth figure to the far right is a man whose genitals are bare and his hands are

tied. Under his head lies a bird mask. Many researchers have suggested that this man is a

prisoner. But more than likely he was an initiate who was about to be circumcised and

inducted into the ranks of *jow* class. This would explain the kuno mask lying under the head of the bound man. In all probability the bound man was to be given this mask after the circumcision rite.

This interpretation of the Chalcatzingo figure, is supported by the fact that each headdress worn by the *jow* (priests) are different. In addition, only two of the three officials on the Chalcatzingo relief wear mask, and even in the case of the mask, the jo-fa nearest the bound man has the most elaborate headdress of all three. This illustrates that the Olmec priestly class was ranked.

Knowledge of the Malinke-Bambara religion can help us understand the significance of the paddles carried by the **Komo** mask wearers. These men were plank bearers (**karaw**). In the traditional religion of the Malinke-Bambara these initiates carry long planks which they exhibit during the ceremonies of the secret society. They illustrate the initiate's identification with the Invisible.

The helmet of the principal Chalcatzingo *jo*, probably the *jo-fa* of Chalcatzingo has three interesting Olmec symbols. They are *tò la gbe*, 'Obedience to the cult is pure virtue'.

Due to the importance of the Olmec cult specialists to Olmec society, the *jo* was recognized as a revered ancestor. The *jo* was considered mediators between man and his god(s), and possessing extensive supernatural powers. The divine status accorded the Olmec rulers and *jow*, especially the **nama-tigi** was so great that it made the graves of these dignitaries repositories of effective talismanic power. This view si made clear by the inscriptions from Offering No.4 from LaVenta, which maintains that the tomb of **Ka Pe ,** was an "effective amulet providing one with virtue".

The cult association was recognized as the major Olmec socializing element. The duties of the priests were to teach the children the laws of Olmec society and obedience to the cult.

Olmec Child Cult Associations

The Olmec child, as evident in Olmec art, was very important in Olmec symbolism. It would appear that the child was recognized as the only representative of the childhood of mankind. The childhood of mankind was the primitive state of man when man was pure and ignorant of nature. This is why we see frequent representations of children as jaguar children, and plumpness characteristic of healthy children, associated with the *jo-fa*. Thus the child in Olmec iconography represents the human being when he left the Creator's hands: uncircumcised and androgynous, possessing in one person the male and female characteristics.

Fig. 3

Olmec children belonged to the **n'domo** brotherhood. This society was open to all Olmec children before circumcision.

Each initiate was given a jo fa, as illustrated by the Las Limas figure. The children of the association were called **tigi-denw** 'children of the tigi', in recognition to the authority of the principle **jo fa** of the **komo** over the members of the cult association.

It is clear from the frequent representation of Children in Olmec art, that children were taken seriously and considered to be able to administer duties which in

most societies were assigned to adults. This suggest that
the members of the **n'domo** were the organizers and
celebrants of their own association functions.

The depiction of children in Olmec art illustrates that
adults respected children. This view is supported by the
motifs on Altar No.5 of LaVenta. On this monument we have a
personage emerging from the stone altar with the glyph
po gbe 'Pure Righteousness' on his headdress. He is
carrying a babe in his arms resting on his lap.

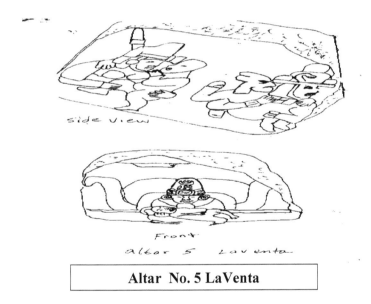

side view

Front
altar 5 LaVenta

Altar No. 5 LaVenta

On the other side of Altar No.5, we find two
personages, each with a different helmet style holding a
child. In each instance the child appears to be in

different poses. In the scene on the left a seated man is holding a limp child on his lap. The child is looking directly at the face of the Olmec dignitary, as if they are engaged in an animated conversation. This scene probably presents the role of the *jo fa* , in instructing the child in the secrets of the society.

In the scene on the right the child appears to wear a headdress, and takes on the mouth of the jaguar. The personage in this scene is standing. He has a snake on his headdress, and is still carrying the child. But instead of carrying the child on his lap, the child is now carried in the personage's arm away to his side. The jaguar child in this scene appears to be offering the Olmec personage instructions on where they should go. This scene suggest that the Olmec child once he graduated from the initiation was recognized as an individual to be respected, and given recognition for his ability to consult with adults.

The Olmec cult associations emphasized the transmission of knowledge from the cult specialists or *jow* , to the young initiates. This view is made vividly clear by numerous Olmec monuments which show a jaguar child in the arms of a helmeted cult-leaders who appears to be instructing, and introducing an Olmec child to the cultural and religious norms of Olmec society. A good example of this phenomenon is Altar No.5 at LaVenta. At Altar No.5 we find a figure emerging from a niche holding a baby in his arms.

The jaguar babies are usually nude and sexless. This suggests that the Olmec initiates into the cult association, were not circumcised and thus androgynous. An another Olmec artifact that illustrates the importance of the cult specialist in Olmec society is the babe-in-arms figurine from Las Limas, Veracruz. The Las Limas figurine has symbols on the head and shoulders of the priest, and headband and chest of the babe.

P.D. Joraleman believes that the incised profile heads on the seated figurine's shoulders represent sky symbols because they are raptorial birds. He believes that the figures on the knees are a shark and serpent and represent the watery world.

Our knowledge of Olmec writing allows us to read the authentic meaning of the glyphs on the babe-in-arms figure. The glyphs on the shoulder represent the bird and jaguar masks cult associations. The eyes on the masks engraved on the shoulder are open and probably represent active force or power.

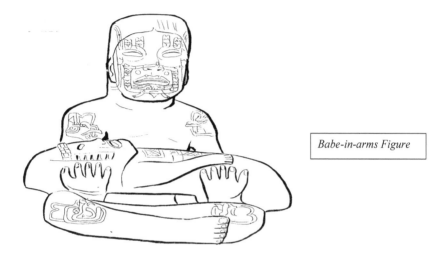

Babe-in-arms Figure

The same masks or cult symbols are also found on the knees of the priest with their eyes closed. They may represent the inactive aspect of the cult symbols when associated with the Olmec children who lack intimate knowledge of the cult association. Symbolically, the mask emblems may mean that the child must obey the **amatigi** from birth to the grave.

The Olmec signs on the face of the priest holding the babe are written in syllabic Olmec script. The glyph on the face   is composed of three signs   **fa**,

a,   **ta**, or **fa-a ta** or " The father is obedient to the order/association".

Olmec Child of the Babe-in-arms figure

Across the headband of the babe we find the glyph or **Po gbe** 'pure virtue'. The glyph across the chest is   .

. This glyph has four signs **bi**,

jo , **po** and **gbe**: **bi jo po gbe**. This means,
'To be consecrated to the cult and pure virtue".

The Olmec children played many specialized roles in
Olmec cult associations. There are many figurines of
children carrying torches, or both torches and knuckle
busters like the jade figurine from San Cristobal
Tepatlaxco, State of Pueblo. These children were called
tatuguw (fire bearers). The **tatuguw** represents the
illumination and purification of the initiate's spirit.

The torch is a very interesting Olmec motif. The term
for torch is **moso**. **Moso**, also means 'master key, magic pass
(built around a person or object), magic charm and magic
passage'. This suggest that the figures from Olmec art
holding torches were assistants to the **nama tigi**, who would

illustrate his high position through wearing the jaguar mask. The torch motif is evident in the jade figure from San Cristobal, Tepatlaxco.

> **Figure San Cristobal, Tepatlaxco**

Another interesting motif associated with the jaguar babies is eyebrows in the form of flames. These flames (**tamla**)probably acknowledge the numinous character of knowledge one learnt in the Olmec cult associations. The depiction of eyebrows in the form of flames probably indicates the illumination one obtains from acquiring knowledge.

Olmec Serpent Worship

The Olmec people also worshipped the serpent or **sa**. The term **sa** can mean serpent, rain, god, and the 'old god' in the Malinke-Bambara language. In fact, it appears that aspects of the serpent are included in the mask of both the bird mask cult and the feline mask cult associations. A good example of this combination of serpent elements with the other cults, is the depiction of a snake on the helmet of the priest on Altar No.5 LaVenta carrying the jaguar baby. Most often, in Olmec art, we find the combination of jaguar and/or bird features mixed with the elements of a serpent.

Stelea no.21 ,from Izapa also record the decline of the Olmec nama and kuno religions and probable raise of the Maya speakers and the sa (serpent) cult which called for human sacrifice. On Stelae no.21, we see a decapitated individual lying on the ground.

An elite carries the decapitated head. This elite wears a new style headdress which resembles the Maya style headdresses.

In the background we see an elite personage being borne in an elaborate sedan chair. Above this chair we see the serpent .

The Izapa, Chiapas figures in Stela 21, indicate the rise of the **sa** cult as a popular cult association among the Olmecs. In this rubbing we see decapitated individuals lying on the ground. An elite carries the decapitated head. This elite wears a new style headdress, which resembles the Maya style headdress.

In the background of Izapa Stela 21, we see a personage being borne in an elaborate sedan chair. Above this chair we see the serpent. This serpent corresponds to the figure in Monument 19 of LaVenta.

In some Olmec iconography such as a sarcophagus at
LaVenta which has a bas-relief of the feline god with a
forked tongue, suggest that the serpent was a minor god
among the early Olmecs (Soustelle,1981). Monument 44 and
Monument 19 of LaVenta also illustrate the serpent cult
among the Olmec.

Monument 19
LaVenta, Mexico

In Monument 19, a seated man wearing a jaguar helmet
has a rattlesnake behind him. This rattlesnake probably
represents the serpent, as the provider of secret knowledge
to his followers, as long as they do not openly share the
source of their knowledge to the uninitiated.

In other parts of the world namely India and Ethiopia, the **sa** cult, is called the **Naga** cult. The worship of Naga was often confined to the intellectual class. This was probably true in Mexico were the bifid tongue associated with serpents was made a part of many ware-jaguar and birdman figurines.

This depiction of a serpent as a background in Izapa Stela 21, corresponds to Monument 19 of La Venta. On Monument 19, from La Venta we see an Olmec personage which has a serpent behind his back and above his head. These depictions of serpents, indicates hidden knowledge or powers from the serpent that the cult leader used to lead the followers of their cult.

Other Olmec Symbolism

There are other aspects of Olmec religion such as the toad, spider and duck motifs, and mirrors. Alison B. Kennedy has made a strong case for the toad in Olmec iconography. The toad was called **tori** or **tote**. The word **tori** also means hammer of the blacksmith. In the Olmec religion the toad probably symbolized death and resurrection of man.

Kennedy believes that the toad was also important to the Olmec priest because of its hallucinogenic or narcotic properties. Due to the narcotic properties of the toad the duck because a major part of Olmec ritual because the duck could press out much of the parotid secretion which is poisonous without harmful effect. The duck's bill was adapted to performing this task.

This gives added significance to the famous Tuxtla statuette of a priest figure wearing a feathered cloak and duckbill mask. This dignitary may have been responsible for the processing of the toad narcotic before rituals.

The appearance of ducks , the spider and following rain are all explained by the Malinke-Bambara traditional religion. As mentioned earlier, the term for rain was **sa or ka**. This is very interesting because these terms are also titles for people of high status. In addition, these terms signify the sky or the region where rain is formed, the divinity of the sky and of the rain and sky diviner in Malinke-Bambara.

The duck in Malinke-Bambara is also called **burr** or **bun**. These terms also mean supreme chief , king or governor. This lends added significance to the Tuxtla statuette which is made in the form of a duck bill man. The Tuxtla statuette contains a funerary inscription for **Ka Tutu** the governor of the Tuxtla settlement.

An interesting African proverb states that "The spider spins his web". This may relate to the Malinke-Bambara tradition of males weaving. According to Bambara traditions, the Supreme god gave weaving and speech to man so he could advance from his primitive state to civilization. The spider spinning his web, is suppose to have inspired man with the idea of weaving.

Mirrors and axes play an important role in Olmec secret societies, just like the Malinke-Bambara secret societies. The mirror in Olmec was called **fere-la**. The term **fere-la** relates to the **nama** society. For example, i n Malinke-Bambara **fere** is the surname of the hyena, and this word Also relates to the magic words used to produce a magic incantation by the traditional Bambara shamans. The term fere may have been transferred to the jaguar, once the Neo-Atlanteans settled in Mexico.

The fact that **fere-la** means mirror, and **fere** relates to important aspects of the **nama** worship, may explain the important role the mirror played in olmec ritual life. It was not only a means of setting a fire in virgin jungle, so the land could be used for agriculture; it also probably was a symbol of the ability of the **nama tigi** to produce magic because it represented the magic key that allowed **tigi** to manipulate the secret forces of heaven and earth.

Axes are also found at Olmec sites in burials or on engravings. The term for axe in Olmec was **yele**. **Yele**, also relates to **nama** worship since the term refers to the snicker of a feline. This tool was very necessary for self-preservation in the bush, so it would be a logical symbol of the **nama tigi** mastery of the bush.

In conclusion , Stela No.5 Izapa provides the story behind the African migration to America. It also gives us a detailed account of the separation of the Olmec religion and people into two major groups. Stela No.5 of Izapa is therefore an important historical document.

It is clear from Olmec iconography and Izapa Stela No.5, that the Olmec religion was made up of two principal **Komow** or secret societies the **nama** or jaguar cult and the **kuno** or bird cult. Each cult was led by a **jo fa** or father of the cult who lead the ceremonies as specific Olmec signs and instructed students in the mysteries of each cult association.

The appearance of children in Olmec art related to the important role the cult association played in socializing youth into Olmec society, and thus creating solidarity within each Olmec community. This made the initiates nobles in relation to the uninitiated members of society.

It should be noted that many of the major Olmec centers were cult centers were youth were initiated into the Olmec secret societies by Olmec *jow* (cult specialists). These centers were places where neophytes were inducted into the **nama** or **kuno komow** . The iconography of the jaguar, and bird were outward manifestations of the Olmec religion. At religious centers like San Lorenzo and LaVenta, youth probably learned the deep mysteries associated with each cult, especially knowledge about the ancient serpent god or **sa**.

In addition to serving as centers of learning, sites such as LaVenta, also served as ceremonial centers, where important rituals were staged and held. Here the rights of diverse **komow** were probably celebrated. At many of these sites famous **nama-tigiw** or **kuno-tigiw** were buried. After the death of great *jo faw* were made into saints. The graves of these saints were recognized as talisman effective in transmitting blessings and righteousness to visitors to the tombs of leading **jow**. For example, Ka-Pe, of LaVenta Offering No.4 was a **nama tigi**, while Ka-Tutu of Tuxtla was probably a **kuno-tigi**. In these inscriptions it was stated that their tombs were talismans where visitors can obtain blessings and grace.

Chapter 10

Olmec Kings

The Olmec inscriptions record the names and deeds of many political officials, religious leaders and Kings (Winters, 1997). The Olmec inscriptions indicate that each Olmec town was ruled by either a governor or King, and that there was a recognized religious leader for the entire community (Winters, 1997).

The Olmec King was usually referred to as *Tu*. The Olmec term for governor was *Ku*. Interestingly, some of the Olmec rulers were referred to as the *Ku* and *Tu*. This may suggest that the Olmec civilization may have been organized into a confederation of city-states lead by a recognized emperor .

The Olmec emperor may have appointed the local government heads or *Ku* (governors). The fact that some Olmec rulers referred to themselves as *Ku Tu*, or both governor and King may reflect the Olmec Emperor's appointment of conquered Kings as governors over Olmec cities they formerly mastered as a result of divine right.

One the most interesting Olmec historical documents is the Mask from Rio Pesquero Veracruz. According to the inscriptions on the mask, it was worn by Bada, who was recognized as the local **Ku** and chief **La** (leader of the stone mason's caste) (Gutherie, 1995: 268, illustration No.186). `

Between 900-600 BC one of the major rulers at Guerrero was Po Ngbe (Gutherie, 1995: 231, illustration No.127). There is also an important tablet from Ahuelican, Guerrero

of mottled green stone that also mentions King Po Ngbe, and his building of a great temple at his site.

One of the most interesting political elites of the Olmec was Bu. Bu is the kneeling figure from Veracruz, known as the "Shaman in Transformation" (Gutherie, 1995: 169-170).

In reading the inscription on the head of this figure, we discover that Bu was a member of the stonemason caste, who later became governor of Veracruz.

The major Epi-Olmec inscriptions have also been deciphered (Winters,1997). Two of the longest Epi-Olmec inscriptions come from Tuxtla .

The Epi-Olmec inscriptions record calendrical dates, in addition to important information on the reigns of Governor TuTu at Tuxtla, and King Yo Pe of Mojarra. Yo Pe was born on 21 May 143 AD, he was recognized as the ruler of Mojarra and also the **Se Gyo** (religious leader with considerable wonder making ability).

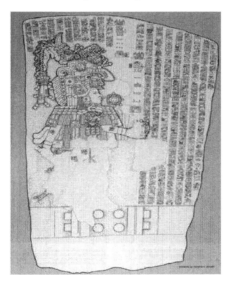

King Yo Pe

Other Epi-Olmec rulers include Ki and Kele. King Ki is buried in tomb 1, at Rio Azul in Guatemala. King Kele, is the ruler buried at Tikal, beneath Structure 5D 33-2nd.

The Olmec polity recognized a unique relationship between the Olmec ruler and his subjects. It is clear that the leader of the Olmec cities were seen as both civil and religious heads.

It would appear from the evidence that the Olmec emperors or **Tu** were usually from the noble class of farmers. The governors or *Ku,* on the other hand were artisans who held the secret knowledge of working stone and wood to produce valuable artifacts that benefited the Olmec society.

The Olmec emperor employed many symbols of their power. The most powerful symbol of the emperor's authority was the various inscribed celts and scepters found at many Olmec centers.

The **La** craft association, performed the tasks of wood carving and monopolized stone work. This probably made the people consider the members of the **la** class to possess special powers because of their responsibility in making tools and sculpting ritual and utilitarian objects of wood and stone.

Very few people probably knew how to work the stone and wood in Olmec land. This ability to perform expert tasks probably made many regular Olmec fear the power of the stone/wood workers. We can assume that the members of the **la** class were trained as doctors, amulet makers, priests and etc.

Chapter 11

The Cascajal Tablet

I claim the Olmecs as Africans because they came from Africa and spoke an African language. The best evidence for African Olmecs is the Cascajal tablet.

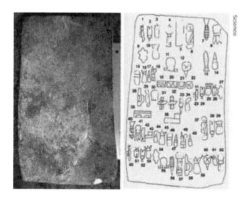

Cascajal Tablet

The Cascajal Tablet according to the road builders at the village where the tablet was found in a mound. The fact that a mound existed where the tablet was found offers considerable support to the idea that the mound where the tablet was found is the tomb of BiPoPo.

The obituary on the Cascajal Tablet may be written about one of the Royals among Olmec heads found at San Lorenzo. The Cascajal Tablet may relate to the personage depicted in San Lorenzo monument 3.

Head 3 San Lorenzo

HEAD 3,
SAN LORENZO
(Monument 3),
1.78 m (5.84 ft) tall.
Jalapa Museum
of Anthropology.

The names of the rulers depicted as the Olmec heads is probably found among the symbols associated with the individual Olmec heads. The headband on monument 3 is made up of four parallel ropes encircling the head. In the parallel ropes there are two serrated figures that cross the ropes diagonally.

There is also a plaited diadem or four braids on the back of the monument 3 covered with serrated element. On the side of the head of monument 3, two serrated elements on four parallel lines hang. This element ends with a three-tiered element hanging.

In the Olmec writing the serrated elements means Bi, while the boxes under the serrated element within the four parallel lines would represent the words PoPo. This suggest that the name for monument 3 was probably BiPoPo.

The hanging element on monument 3 is similar to one of the signs on the Cascajal tablet. Although symbol 57 on the Cascajal monument is hard to recognize it appears to include the Bi sign on the top of the symbol. This finding indicates that the BiPoPo of monument 3, is most likely the BiPo(Po) mentioned in the Cascajal Tablet.

Cascajal Sign 57

57

The Meso-American archaeologist Stirling said that monument 3 was found at the bottom of a deep ravine half-a-mile southwest of the principal mound of San Lorenzo, along with ceramic potsherds. This is interesting because the village of Cascajal is situated southwest of San Lorenzo.

According to reports of the discovery of the road builders who found the Cascajal Tablet, the tablet came from a mound at Cascajal which was located about a mile from San Lorenzo. The coincidence of finding San Lorenzo Monument 3 in the proximity of the Cascajal mound where the Cascajal Tablet was found suggest that these artifacts concern the same personage. This leads to the possibility that the Cascajal mound was the tomb of BiPoPo.

All the evidence indicates that the Cascajal Tablet is an obituary for a Olmec ruler named BiPoPo.

Given the presence of similar signs on the Olmec

head called San Lorenzo monument 3, which also read

BiPoPo suggest that the Cascajal Tablet was written

for the personage depicted in Olmec head 3.

Head 3 San Lorenzo

HEAD 3,
SAN LORENZO
(Monument 3),
1.78 m (5.84 ft) tall.
Jalapa Museum
of Anthropology.

If the Cascajal Tablet really corresponds to

one of the Olmec heads suggest that Cascajal may

have been a royal burial site. If this is the case
it is conceivable that other tablets relating to
Olmec rulers may also be found at this locale,
since some of these other mounds may be the
"hemispheric" tombs of other Olmec rulers.

The Olmec signs are homophones. This means
that each sign can have multiple meanings. The
first thing you do is check the list of syllabic
signs already identified.

This is list of Olmec signs. You can use these signs to read any Olmec inscription.

After this you compare the target sign and the

Olmec syllabic signs. If you don't recognize a
particular sign from the list, you may want to
refer back to the list of Vai signs provided by
Delafosse.

Certain signs in the Cascajal stela/tablet
appear multiple times.

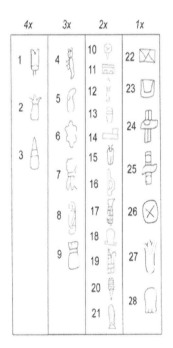

The Olmec writing on the Cascajal tablet is an
obituary for King Bi Po. This writing is written in
Hieroglyphic Olmec (Winters,2006). Hieroglyphic
Olmec includes multiple linear Olmec signs which
are joined together to make pictures of animals,
faces and other objects.

Some researchers have recognized insects and

other objects in the signs. In reality these signs are made up several different Olmec linear signs as noted above when they are broken down into their elements.

The Olmec writing is read right to left top to bottom. Each segment of the Olmec sign has to be broken down into its individual syllabic sign. In most cases the Olmec signs includes two or more syllabic characters. The Olmec signs can be interpreted as follows:

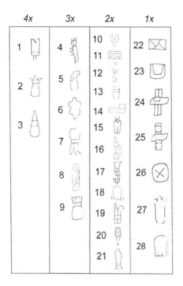

To read the various Cascajal Inscriptions you have
to separate each sign into its syllabic element.
Once this is done you can read the inscription.

Transliteration of the Cascajal Signs

- 1. La fe ta gyo

2. Bi yu

3. Pa po yu

4. Se ta I su

5. Ta kye

6. Beb be

7. Bi Po Yu to

8. Tu fa ku

9. Tu pa pot u

10. Ta gbe pa

11. i-tu

12. Bi Yu yo po

13. Kye gyo

14. Po lu

15. Fe ta yo i

16. Be kye

17. Fe gina

18. Po bi po tu

19. Lu kye gyo to

20. Kye tu a pa

21. Yu gyo i

22. Pa ku pa

23. Po yu

24. Day u kye da

25. Po ta kye tap o

26. Ta gbe

27. Bi Fa yu

28. Bi Yu / Paw

Translation

Reading the Cascajal Tablet from right to left we have the following:

- (8) Bi Po lays in state in the tomb, (7) desiring to be endowed with mysterious faculties.

  (6) This abode is possessed by the Governor .

  (5)…. (4) Bi Po Po.

  (3) Bi (was), (2) an Artisan desires to be consecrated to the divinity. (1) (and He)

merits thou offer of libations.

(14). Admiration (for) the cult specialist's hemisphere tomb. (13) The inheritance of thou vital spirit is consecration to the divinity.

(12) In a place of righteous admiration, (11) Pure Bi (in a) pure abode

(10) A pure mark of admiration (is) this hemispheric tomb.

(9) [Here] lays low (the celebrity) [he] is gone.

(22) The place of righteousness, [is] (21) the pure hemispheric tomb

(20)

(19) Thou (art) obedient to the Order. (18) Hold upright the Order (and) the divinity of the sacred cult.

(17) Pure Admiration this place of, (16) Bi the Vital Spirit. (15) [Truly this is] a place consecrated to the divinity and propriety.

27) Lay low (the celebrity) to go to , (26) love the mystic order—thou vivid image of the race,

(25) The pure Govenor and (24) Devotee [of the Order lies in this] hemispheric tomb ,desires [to be] a talisman effective in providing one with virtue, (23) [He] merits thou offer of Libations.

(34) Command Respect. (33)….this place of admiration. (32) Thou sacred inheritance is propriety. (31) The Govenor commands existence in a unique state, (31) [in] this ruler's hemispheric tomb. (29) The Royal (28) [was] a vigorous man.

(36) The pure habitation (35) [of a]Ruler obedient to the Order.

(37) This abode is possessed by the governor.

(38) Admiration to you [who art] obedient to the Order.

(49) Pure admiration [for this] tomb.

(48) Thou hold upright the pure law.

(47). Pure admiration [for this tomb].

(46) [It] acts [as] a talisman effective in providing one with virtue.

(45) Bi Po, (44) a pure man, (43) of wonder, (42) [whose] inheritance is consecration to the Divinity.

(41) Bi Po lays in state in the tomb, (40) desiring to be endowed with mysterious faculties.

(62) Bi Po lays in state in the tomb.

(61) [This] tomb [is a] sacred object, (60) a place of righteous wonder.

(59) Bi's tomb (58) [is in] accord [with] the law (57) Bi exist in a unique (and) pure state the abode of the Govenor is pure..

(56) The inheritance of [this] Ruler is joy.

(55) [In] this tomb of King Bi (54) lays low a celebrity, [he] is gone.

(53) The tomb of Bi (52) is a dormitory [of]

love. A place consacreted to the divinity.

(51) Thou the vivid image of the race love(d)
the mystic order.

(50) [He] merits [your] offer of Libations.

This translation of the Cascajal tablet makes
it clear that the tablet was written for a local
ruler at San Lorenzo called Bi Po. This tablet
indicates that Bi Po's tomb was recognized as a
sacred site. It also indicates that the Olmecans
believed that if they offered libations at the
tombs of their rulers they would gain blessings.

There are other mounds at Cascajal. There is
the possibility that other writings might be found
in the same locale and we may learn the identities
of even more Olmec rulers at San Lorenzo.

References Relating to African Inscriptions:

M. Delafosse, Vai leur langue et leur ysteme

d'ecriture,L'Anthropologie, 10 (1910).

Lambert, N. (1970). Medinet Sbat et la
Protohistoire de Mauritanie Occidentale, Antiquites
Africaines, 4, pp.15-62.

Lambert, N. L'apparition du cuivre dans les
civilisations prehistoriques. In C.H. Perrot et al
Le Sol, la Parole et 'Ecrit (Paris: Societe
Francaise d'Histoire d'Outre Mer) pp.213-226.

R. Mauny, Tableau Geographique de l'Ouest Afrique
Noire. Histoire et Archeologie (Fayard);

Kea,R.A. (2004). Expansion and Contractions: World-
Historical Change and the Western Sudan World-
System (1200/1000BC-1200/1250A.D.) Journal of
World-Systems Research, 3, pp.723-816

Winters, Clyde. (1998). The Decipherment of the

Olmec Writing System. Retrieved 09/25/2006 at

http://olmec98.net/Rtolmec2.htm

Winters,Clyde.(2006). The Olmec Hieroglyphic

Script. Retrieved 09/25/2006 at:

http://olmec98.net/hieromec.pdf

Chapter 12

The Olmec Calendar

The Olmec introduced the calendar to the Meso-Americans. Leo Wiener *in Africa and the Discovery of America* was the first to recognize this fact. Leo Wiener was talking about the sacre calendar of the Maya called *Tzolk'in*.

Leo Wiener, in *Africa and the Discovery of America* discussed the fact that the West African zodiacs are of 13 months like that of the Amerindians 5 . This information is based on the work of F.Bork 6 .

Wiener wrote: "In the first place, the central square contains the Mandingo tutelary god with his attributes and appurtenances. The numerical

5 Leo Wiener, in *Africa and the Discovery of America*, Vol.3, p.279.
6 F.Bork, Tierkreise auf westafrikanischen Kalebassen, in *Mitteilungen der vorderasiatischen Gesellschaft*, Vol.21, p.266.

calculations based on 20 and 13, which is the essence of the American calendars, is surely built on African models. Here again we possess but the scantiest material for verification, but just enough to be startling and unique" 7 .

The Olmec or Mande calendrics are the result of a combination of climatic, social and astronomical factors. The moon, seasons and stars are used for reckoning time. The major star studied by the Mande is Sirius.

The Mande have several calendars, lunar, ritual and etc. The Mande system of notation is based on 20, 60 and 80 according to M. Griaule & G.Dieterlen.

Aspects of the Mande notation system is found among most West Africans. Griaule in **Signes grapheques des Dogon**, made it clear that the number 80 also represented 20 (80÷20=20; 20 x 4=80) and probably relates to the Mande people8 .

7 Weiner, p.270
8 R. Temple, **The Sirius Mystery**, (1976) p.80.

The base of the Mande calculation is 60 (60÷20=3; 3x20=60). The Malinke-

Bambara term for 20 is *muġa* . The Malinke-Bambara term for 60 is *debé ni- muġa* or 40+20 (=60).

Today the Mande Muslims use the Islamic calendar. As a result, we have to look at non-Muslim Mande people and their associates to discover the original calendar of the Mande/Olmec people.

The Dogon claim they got their calendric system from the Mande. The importance of the number 20 is evident in the discussion of the trajectory of the star Digitaria around Serius, as illustrated in Figure iii, above. Note the small cluster of 22 dots (DL) in the figure that represent the star when it is furtherest from Sirius 9 .

---

9 Ibid., p.40.

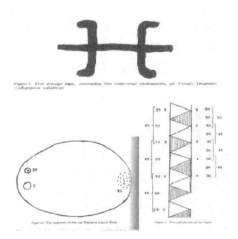

In this figure of **Kanaga sign** above the egg shaped figure which represents Sirius, illustrates the base notation 20 and 60. The head, tail and four feet each represent 20 ,i.e., 6 x 20=120; 120÷60=2.

The calculation of Sigui also indicates the Mande notation system of 20 and 60.

Further confirmation of the base 20 notation in relation to the Sirius system is the **kosa wala**. For example on the koso wala we have 10 sequences made up of 30 rectangles (10x30 =300), which can be divided by 20: 300÷20=15; and 60: 300÷60=5. And as noted by Griaule & Dieterlen in addition to the above, 20 reactangles in the **koso wala** represent stars and constellations10 .

The Mayan system like the Mande system is also based on 60 and 20. For example, the basic part of the **Haab** year is the **Tun** 18 month 20 day calendar, plus the five day month of **Wayeb**.The basic unit of the calendar is the Tun made up of 18 winal (months) of 20 k'in (days) or 360 days.

Thus we have 18x20=360; 360÷60=6.Next we have the **K'tun**,(20 Tun) which equals 7200 days, 7200÷60=120÷60=2; or 7200÷20=360÷20=18.After K'tun comes **Baktun** (=400 Tun) 144,000 days, 144,000÷60=2400÷60=40; or 144,000÷20=7200÷20= 360÷20=18. Yes the Mande had the zero.

---

10 Ibid., p.48.

The Mayan symbol for 'zero' means completion. M. Griaule in **Signes d'Ecriture Bambara**, says the Malinke-Bambara sign for zero is *fu* 'nothing, the emptiness preceding creation' 11 .

In summary, Mayan calendrics are probably based on the Mande notation system of 20 and 60. And the Olmec and other Malinke-Bambara people possessed the zero.

Mayan groups record successfully time only using the 13 month 20 day calendar so there was no need for the Olmec to record a date and use a system like the *Haab* (*Tun+ Wayeb*) to determine its actual time. A similar calendar of 13 months and 20 days was recorded on West African calabashes ..

The Mayan name for day *k'in,* is of Olmec/Mande origin it agrees with the Malinke-Bambara term *kenè* that means 'day light, day'. The Mayan term for series of 360 days is tun, this corresponds to the Mande term *dõ-na* 'an arrangement of dates/days',

---

11 , Marcel Griaule & Germaine Dieterlen, **Signes graphique soudanais**.

the Olmec term for calendar is probably the Mande

word *dõ-gyãle-la*.

The Mayan speakers probably used *tun*, because

they learned the Mande calendar in association with

ritual days of the Mande speaking Olmecs..

Lets recap Wiener noted the existence of 13

month 20 day zodiacs in West Africa, and the

American sacre calendar is made up of 20 days and

13 months. Coe and Montgomery says the 13 month

260-day calendar continues to be used in Guatemala

and other cultures up to today.

The Mande Kosa Wala and Mayan Calendrics

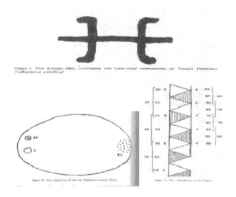

The Mande clanedrics are related to the Sirius system. Further confirmation of the base 20 notation in relation to the Sirius system is the **kosa wala** . For example on the koso wala we have 10 sequences made up of 30 rectangles (10x30 =300), which can be divided by 20: 300÷20=15; and 60: 300÷60=5. And as noted by Griaule & Dieterlen in addition to the above, 20 reactangles in the **koso wala** represent stars and constellations 12 .

It is interesting that when Griaule and Dieterlen, discussed the Mande notation system they used a (colored blanket) **wala koso**, while the Mande linguistic expert Delafosse used the example of a (mat) **degè**, in the Mande notation system. This suggest that the ancient Mande used mats to perform math computation and that these mats were made according to the base 20 notation system.

The Olmec calendar is where we get the Calendar Round. Coe and Stone, **Reading the Maya Glyphs** wrote : "The first part of a Calendar Round

12 Temple, **The Sirius Mystery** , p.48.

is the 260-day Count, often called in the literature by the ersatz Maya name **"*tsolk'in*"**. This is the eternally repeating cycle , and consist of the numbers 1 through 13, permuting against a minicycle of 20 named days. Since 13 and 20 have no common denominator, a particular day name will not recur with a particular coefficient until 260 days have passed. No one knows exactly when this extremely sacred calendar was invented, but it was certainly already ancient by the time the Classic period began. There are still highland Maya calendar priests who can calculate the day in the 260-day Count, and it is apparent that this basic way of time-reckoning has never slipped a day since its inception" (pp.41-42).

Coe and Stone, **Reading the Maya Glyphs** wrote : "The first part of a Calendar Round is the 260-day Count, often called in the literature by the ersatz Maya name "tsolk'in". This is the eternally repeating cycle , and concist of the numbers 1

through 13, permuting against a minicycle of 20
named days. Since 13 and 20 have no common
denominator, a particular day name will not recur
with a particular coefficient until 260 days have
passed. No one knows exactly when this extremely
sacred calendar was invented, but it was certainly
already ancient by the time the Classic period
began. **There are still highland Maya calendar**
priests who can calculate the day in the 260-day
Count, and it is apparent that this basic way of
time-reckoning has never slipped a day since its
inception" (pp.41-42).

This sacre Meso-American calendar has 13
months of 20 days (13x20=260). John Montgomery, ***How***
to Read Maya Hieroglyphs, wrote "The ***Tzolk'in*** or
260 day Sacred Almanac, was widely used in ancient
times for divinatory purposes. **Guatemalan Maya and**
other cultures in Mexico still use it as a means of
"day keeping". The origins of the 260-day calendar
are debatable although a number of scholars have

suggested it corresponds to the nine month period of human gestation" (p.74).

As you can see Maya experts don't know where this calendar originated. Dr. Wiener, as an astute scholars suggested that it originated in Africa, where we see the 13 month zodiac calabashes.

Ignacio Bernal, in **The Olmec World** explains the two methods Mayanist use to interpret Maya dates. Bernal explains that Mayanists use two correlations to make the Meso-American calendar agree with the Western calendar. Bernal claims that the MesoAmerican calendar dates back to 4 October 3373, if you use Correlation A of the Maya Long Count. American scholars, on the other hand use the correlation B date of 13 August 3114 to determine Maya dates using the Maya Long Count .

To determine dates relating to the Maya Long Count researchers need to know Mayan initial series signs. The Olmecs did not use initial series signs to write their calendar dates. This can lead to confusion determing Olmec dates. This confusion results from the absence of an Olmec initial series sign which would accurately assign a date to a particular period.

Using correlation A, if the Olmec dot and bar signs were long count dates would situate the Epi-Olmec during the late Olmec period. It is obvious that the dates assigned Epi-Olmec text may be too late and is used to make it appear that there was a break in continuity between Epi-Olmec and the classical Olmec. It is too late to get Carbon 14 dates for the Mojarra and Tuxtla artifacts, but it is clear that we need to look at these artifacts to accurately date and verify that the dot and bars found on the Epi-Olmec text correspond to carbon 14 dates for materials found in association with Epi-Olmec text.

Below is an Olmec artifact from Chiapas de Corzo stela number 2 (wall panel).

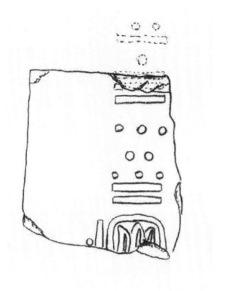

Experts will go to great lengths to make up dates.
For example,in relation to the Chiapa de Corzo
stela 2 (wall panel) found by the NWAF. Researchers
decided that the "stela" probably represented a
date so they hypothesized that the date for the
monument was 7 16 3 2 18, because they felt it was
similar to the "calendrial pattern" of the Tuxtla
statuette, Stela C and etc; eventhough we only
visibly see 10 3 2 18. This date is recognized as
the earliest Epi-Olmec dated artifact.

To determine Maya dates you have to know the initial series signs. The Olmec calendar scholars did not use the initial series to write Olmec dates.

The best example of the lack of Olmec initial series signs on Olmec monuments is the Mojarra stela.

The Mojarra steal was written in honor of King Yo Pe. In the inscription we are told the date King Yo Pe was born . Just because this was a date does not take away the fact that dots and bars can also represent lexical items in the Olmec language as we discussed in the Chapter on Olmec writing.

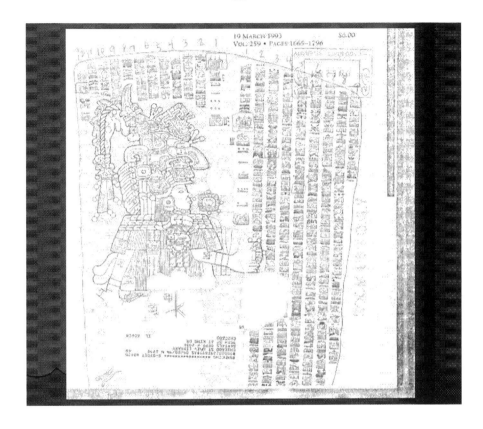

I have already deciphered and published the side Mojarra inscription. Now I will decipher the face of the Mojarra stela.

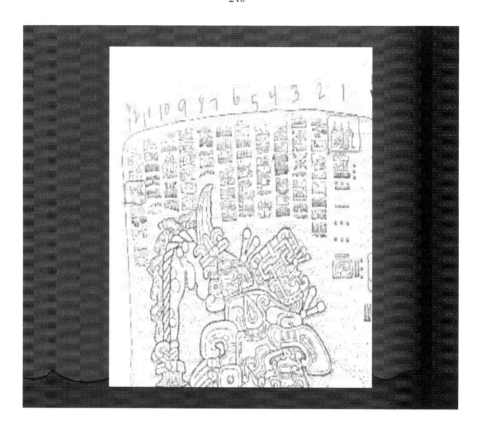

The first column of the Mojarra inscription reads
as follows:

Row 1 (reading right to left).

(1) i ta ki yo. (1a) i po Ki se. (1b) i ta
ki yo.

1/1b. Thou sacre raising (as) a vital
spirit exist (now).

1a. Thou the pure Protector / or You (art)
Pure Kise.

2) Ba da Yo

The Great Da Yo.

3. Se po Da Yo

The victorious and Pure Da Yo

4. Po tu

Pure birth (was on)

5. 8 5 3 3 5

May 21 ,143 AD

6. Se Gyo

(Thou art) Se gyo

 Snake

(Se gyo is a surname given to an enfant whose people ascribe the intervention of a divinity.)

"Thou sacre raising exist (now). Thou (art) the Pure Protector. The Great Da Yo. The victorious and pure Da Yo's pure birth (was on) May 21 143 AD. Thou (art) the Se Gyo. Thou Snake"

Row 2

Ni Po
Kyu gyo
Po tu
Yo po bo po ta
Monkey Tu
Yo
pa po
Ta
Se lu la
Tu ku tu
Yo Pe

" (1)The pure house, (2)the big hemisphere sepulcre (burial Pyramid?) is a talisman. (3)Pure King Yo, is pure moral gradeur (and) a pure Propriety. (4) The Monkey King. (5) Yo (6) has much purity (7) the devotee is pure. (8) To realize and hold upright a good situation. (9) The king and Governor is obedient to the law. (10) (Oh) Yo Pe."

```
Po tu
Pe pe Ngbe
Yo Pe
Papa Po gbe Papa
Yo Pe
Pe po pe
Da Yo da
```

"The pure King (he has) Prodigious purity
and virtue. The pure Yo, very much purity
and virtue (is due) Yo Pe. Very much
admiration for Da Yo at this moment the
king."

```
lu ma tu gyo
Yo Pe
```

"Hold upright spiritual tranquility for
the ruler and cult leader: Yo Pe."

The first date relates to the birth of Yo Pe
who was recognized **as Se Gyo**. The inscription makes
it clear that Yo Pe was recognized as a god and the
leader of his people's religion.

To understand the designation of *Yo Pe as Se
Gyo* (Se Jo) is explained by Mande traditional
culture. As I said earlier I made a mistake and
transliterated Pe gyo, as Se gyo. Reading the signs

as Pe gyo tells us that Yo Pe was considered a powerful religious specialist in addition to be the King.

I do not believe the "loopy" sign was an Initial Series character. It was just a description of the potent supernatural power Yo Pe possessed.

Se gyo, Yo Pe appears to have had great knowledge of sorcery or **nyama**. **Se** (foot, foundation) represents the beginning of knowledge. The se symbolizes beginning, an advance of success and power. The se represents man's progression in pursuit of knowledge. Since Se, means foundation and gyo, is spiritual knowledge. **Se gyo** would = **"foundation of spiritual knowledge"**.

Nyama is occult power or special energy of supernatural origin. Nyama is considered source of power behind every task. Among the Mande the pinnacle of potency is the knowledge of sorcery. Sorcery is important among the Mande says McNaughton because "for the vast majority [of

Mande] sorcery provide a means for analyzing situations and a tool for responding to them, and these people can be quite open about their use of it" (p.13).

P.R. McNaughton's The Mande Blacksmiths: Knowledge, Power and Art in West Africa, gives us keen insight into Mande traditional beliefs and helps explain much of Olmec social concepts and religion. In the Friday transliteration of the signs I gave the following interpretation:

(1) i ta ki yo. (1a) i po Ki se. (1b) i ta ki yo.

1/1b. Thou sacre raising (as) a vital spirit exist (now).

1a. Thou the pure Protector / or You (art) Pure Kise.

Instead of translating this middle sign as i po ki
se, I believe it should read i po kilisi. In the
decipherment of the loopy sign I failed to include
transliteration of the dot sign: li. The lexical
item li, is represented by the black dot inside the
middle symbol. Since "li" is in the middle of the
figure I am reading the se sign as si, instead of
se, thus we have *Kilisi*. Reading the signs as
follows i po kilisi, we have "Thou pure secret
speech".

Kilisi means secret speech. Kilisi is a potent
formula of human sounds rich with supernatural
energy. It is kilisi that provides an object with
nyama.

In relation to the serpent/snake in the
inscription it does not relate to a date. Before
the *sa* or snake we have *se gyo* "Foundation of
spiritual knowledge". I believe that Ye Po was a
Satigi[/]: Master of Snakes.

Among the Mande the snake is used in divination. The snake diviner studies the reptiles movements which he mystically interprets to answer clients questions. The Satigi, communicated with snakes for numerous purposes, e.g., to forsee future events and obtain secret knowledge, because he shares a supernatural bond with the serpent. The Satigi is recognized as one of the most powerful diviners of the Mande people who has the ability to perform supernatural acts (McNaughty, p.52).

This suggest that Se gyo Sa (Snake) may be interpreted as The Se Gyo and Sa(tigi).

In Row 2 we read the following:

- Row 2

    Ni Po
    Kyu gyo
    Po tu
    Yo po bo po ta
    Monkey Tu

```
Yo
pa po
Ta
Se lu la
Tu ku tu
Yo Pe
```

" (1)The pure house, (2)the big hemisphere sepulcre (burial Pyramid?) is a talisman. (3)Pure King Yo, is pure moral gradeur (and) a pure Propriety. (4) The Monkey King. (5) Yo (6) has much purity (7) the devotee is pure. (8) To realize and hold upright a good situation. (9) The king and Governor is obedient to the law. (10) (Oh) Yo Pe."

The monkey figure probably has an important meaning in this inscription and may represent an emblem. Among the Mande **sulaw** monkeys indicates the initiates awareness of his own animality. This suggest that **Sula tu** in row 2, should read "A king aware of his animality".

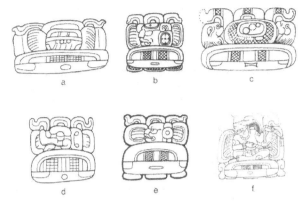

Fig. 3-7 Examples of the Initial Series Introducing Glyph: a) with patron of the month Sek; b) with patron of the month Yaxk'in; c) with patron of the month Ch'en; d) with patron of the month Yax; e) with patron of the month Mol; f) with full-figure patron of the month Mak.

Above are initial series glyphs. If you notice carefully we find that the initial series glyphs usually include the tun (T548 often worn on the head of number '5') main sign, along with a superfix of scrolls and two comb like figures, flanked by a pair of fish or fish fins. Between these signs is situated either a deity, a glyph or a glyph combination, which is the patron god of the month in the Haab.

None of the features of the Initial Series signs *tun* sign scrolls or two comb figures are found in the Majorra stela .

In conclusion it is safe to say that Yo Pe had immense supernatural power, thus his nickname *"Se Gyo"*. He was also a *Satigi*, and thus could see into the future and obtain supernatural knowledge via his snake totem. As a result of this I do not believe that *Se gyo* Snake, is a day sign. These signs probably related to the immense supernatural powers of Yo Pe.

I know the requirements of the Long Count because I studied Mayan hierogyphics under J. Kathryn Josserand and Nicholas A. Hopkins so I have a pretty good understanding of Maya Hieroglyphs and know that the Initial Series is important in finding the date of a monument. Here is a worksheet

we had to do that points out aspects of the Initial

Series.

This worksheet shows that the ISIG is made up of

several parts. If there is an ISIG on the Mojarra

Stela it should have these parts.

Below I present the Mayan ISIGs.

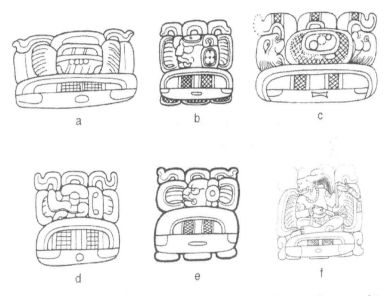

Fig. 3-7   Examples of the Initial Series Introducing Glyph: a) with patron of the month Sek; b) with patron of the month Yaxk'in; c) with patron of the month Ch'en; d) with patron of the month Yax; e) with patron of the month Mol; f) with full-figure patron of the month Mak.

Cursory examination of the Mojarra loopy sign
and the ISIGs above show no affinity. As a result,I
disagree with you, Coe and the others.

The ISIGs published above do not correspond to
the symbols on the Mojarra stela. As a result I do
not believe this "loopy sign" on the Mojarra stela
was an ISIG.

Mojarra Loopy Sign

The ISIGs published above do not correspond to the symbols on the Mojarra stela. As a result I do not believe this was an ISIG.

Below is my interpretation of the loopy sign above.

- **(1) i ta ki yo.(1a) i po Kilise. (1b) i-ta ki yo.**

  1/1b. Thou sacre raising (as) a vital spirit exist (now).

  1a. "Thou pure secret speech

Kilisi means secret speech. Kilisi is a potent formula of human sounds rich with supernatural energy. It is kilisi that provides an object with nyama.

In relation to the serpent/snake in the

inscription it does not relate to a date. Before the *sa* or snake we have **se gyo** "Foundation of spiritual knowledge". I believe that Ye Po was a *Satigi*: Master of Snakes.

Among the Mande the snake is used in divination. The snake diviner studies the reptiles movements which he mystically interprets to answer clients questions. The *Satigi*, communicated with snakes for numerous purposes, e.g., to forsee future events and obtain secret knowledge, because he shares a supernatural bond with the serpent. The *Satigi* is recognized as one of the most powerful diviners of the Mande people who has the ability to perform supernatural acts .

This suggest that *Se gyo Sa (Snake)* may be interpreted as **The Se Gyo and Sa(tigi)**.

It is safe to say that Yo Pe had immense supernatural power, thus his nickname "Se Gyo". He was also a Satigi, and thus could see into the future and obtain supernatural knowledge via his

snake totem. As a result of this I do not believe
that Se gyo Snake, is a day sign. These signs
probably related to the immense supernatural powers
of Yo Pe.

Understanding the Tzolk'in or sacred calendar
is important in understanding why the Mojarra
monument can have a date on it without necessarily
having an initial series introductory glyph (ISIG).
The ISIG announces that the Long Count and Calendar
Round will follow.

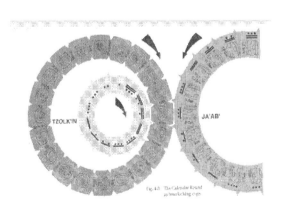

Fig. 4-3. The Calendar Round
34 Interlocking cogs

In the illustration above we have the

components of the Calendar Round. The first part of this process is Tzolk'in sacred calendar. Any date determined by the Tzolk'in can then be converted into the Ja'ab calendar of 20 days and 18 months. Thus we have the interlocking cogs of the Tzolk'in and Ja'ab calendars.

It has been made clear that you can arrive at a reliable date using just the Tzolk'in calendar which existed prior to the invention of the Ja'ab. This is supported by the continued use of Tzolk'in by Americans throughout Meso-America.

The Olmec dates are made up usually of the bar and dot pattern, without the ISIG. Even without the ISIG researchers have determined reliable dates for the Olmec artifacts. This suggest that using Tzolk'in you can determine a date without employing an ISIG. This is why I maintain that the loopy sign is a lexical items, rather than the ISIG.

Final Word

The Olmecs were neo-Atlanteans from Africa. They called themselves Xi (Shi).

The Xi founded a civilization in Mexico, which was imitated by many of the later civilizations of Mexico, including the Maya.

The ancestors of the Olmec had already used jade or amazonite to create artifacts in Africa. They also made giant stone heads of there leaders as tall as 3 feet in Ivory Coast and Senegal, West Africa.

The Native American traditions recorded by Landa, the Mixe-Zoque and Sahagun make it clear that the Mayan and Aztec were not the first people to inhabit the area associated with Olmec archaeology. These traditions claim that the ancient Olmec or Xi people, came from across the Atlantic, and spread throughout Mexico. The Olmec settlers of this area spoke a Manding language closely related to Malinke-Bambara.

The Manding speaking Olmec people, according to Mexican tradition came to Mexico in twelve waves of immigrants around 1200 B.C. As discussed in chapter two this tradition was recorded in Izapa Stela 5.

The Olmecs came from the Saharan zone of North Africa (Winters, 1983, 1984c, 1986), they left the area as it became arid. In Africa, Neo-Atlantean ancestors of the Olmec, left their earliest inscriptions at Oued Mertoutek (Winters, 1979,1983), and jade (amazonite) artifacts throughout Saharan Africa. They took a full-fledged literate culture to Mexico. A culture and civilization which was created to reflect the new living conditions they found in the jungles of Mexico.

This view is supported both by 1) our ability to read the Olmec inscriptions; 2) confirmation that the Mayan term for writing *c'ib, is of Manding origin i.e., **sebe**; 3) the symbols for Olmec writing, found on many Olmec artifacts are cognate to the Manding writing systems used in Africa; and 4) skeletons of Africans found at Olmec sites.

The discovery at Olmec sites such as LaVenta Offering No.4 , of Manding writing provides the "absolute proof " of Neo-Atlantean-African and Olmec contact. The presence of readable African writing on Olmec celts, masks and statues, is the genuine African artifact found "in controlled excavations in the New World" that confirms the claims of

Wiener, Sertima, Sitchin and others that ancient Africans formed a major segment of the Olmec population.

The existence of African writing on Olmec artifacts is confirmation of the Neo-Atlantean influence among the Olmecs (Winters, 1979, 1997). It is a historical fact that fails to minimizes the role of Native Americans as actors in their own history, because the Neo-Atlantean Africanized Olmec people had their own civilization, while the Aztecs and Mayas had theirs. This view of ancient American history , which recognizes a Neo-Atlantean-African role in the rise of Olmec civilization, instead of denigrating Native Americans acknowledges the truth, that all three civilizations made their own unique contributions to the great ancient history of Meso-America.

Appendix

Influence of Olmec Writing on the Mayan Writing

The Olmecs probably founded writing in the Mexico. Dr. Coe, in "Olmec Jaguar and Olmec Kings" (1968), suggested that the beliefs of the Maya were of Olmec origin and that the pre Maya were Olmecs (1968,p.103). This agreed with Brainerd and Sharer's, The ancient Maya (1994,p.65) concept of colonial Olmec at Maya sites. Moreover, this view is supported by the appearance of jaguar stucco mask pyramids (probably built by the Olmecs) under Mayan pyramids e.g., Cerros Structure 5-C-2nd, Uxaxacatun pyramid and structure 5D-22 at Tikal. This would conform to Schele and Freidel's belief that the monumental structures of the Maya were derived from Olmec prototypes.

An Olmec origin for many PreClassic Maya sites, would explain the cover-up of the jaguar stucco mask pyramids with classic Maya pyramids at these sites. It would also explain Schele and Freidel's (1990) claim that the first king of Palenque was the Olmec leader U-Kix-chan; and that the ancient Maya adopted many Olmec social institutions and Olmec symbolic imagery.

The Olmecs spoke and aspect of the Manding (Malinke-Bambara) language spoken in West Africa (Winters, 1979, 1980, 1981,1984).

B. Stross (1973) mentions the Mayan tradition for a foreign origin of Mayan writing. This idea is also confirmed by Mayan oral tradition (Tozzer, 1941), and C.H. Brown (1991) who claimed that writing did not exist among the Proto-Maya.

Terrence Kaufman has proposed that the Olmec spoke a Mexe-Zoquean speech and therefore the authors of Olmec writing were Mexe-Zoquean speakers. This view fails to match the epigraphic evidence. The Olmec people spoke a Manding (Malinke-Bambara) language and not Zoquean.

There is a clear African substratum for the origin of writing among the Maya (Wiener, 1922). All the experts agree that the Olmec people gave the Maya people writing (Schele & Freidel, 1990; Soustelle, 1984). Mayanist also agree that the Proto-Maya term for writing was *c'ihb' or *c'ib'.

Figure 1. Mayan Terms for Writing

Yucatec c'i:b'   Chorti c'ihb'a   Mam   c'i:b'at

Lacandon c'ib'   Chol c'hb'an   Teco   c'i:b'a

Itza   c'ib'   Chontal c'ib'   Ixil   c'ib'

Mopan   c'ib'   Tzeltalan c'ib'

Proto-Term for write *c'ib'

The Mayan /c/ is often pronounced like the hard Spanish /c/ and has a /s/ sound. Brown (1991) argues that *c'ihb may be the ancient Mayan term for writing but, it cannot be Proto-Mayan because writing did not exist among the Maya until 600 B.C. This was 1500 years after the break up of the Proto-Maya (Brown, 1991). This means that the Mayan term for writing was probably borrowed by the Maya from the inventors of the Mayan writing system.

Landa supports the linguistic evidence (Tozzer, 1941) that the Mayan language was introduced to the Maya by non-Mayan speakers. Landa noted that the Yucatec Maya claimed that they got writing from a group of foreigners called **Tutul Xiu** from Nonoulco (Tozzer, 1941).

The **Tutul Xi** were probably Manding speaking Olmecs. The term **Tutul Xiu**, can be translated using Manding as follows:

Tutul[13], "Very good subjects of the Order".

Xiu[14], "The Shi (/the race)".

"The Shis (who) are very good Subjects of the cult-Order".

The term **Shi**, is probably related to the Manding terms Sye or **Si,** which was also used as an ethnonym.

The Mayan term for writing is derived from the Manding term

*se'be. Below are the various terms for writing used by the Manding/Mande people for writing.

Figure 2.<u>Manding Term for Writing</u>

Malinke   se'be   Serere safe

Bambara   se'be   Susu se'be

Dioula   se'we'   Samo se'be

Sarakole   safa   W. Malinke safa

Proto-Term for writing *se'be , *safâ

Brown has suggested that the Mayan term c'ib' diffused from the Cholan and

Yucatecan Maya to the other Mayan speakers. This term is probably derived from

---

[13]. This final –l element , in Tutu-l, is probably the suffix of augmentation.

[14]. The –u or -w, element is the plural suffix for the Manding languages.

Manding *Se'be which is analogous to *c'ib'. This would explain the identification of the

Olmec or Xi/Shi people as Manding speakers.

References

Belyi, V.V. (1997). Rafinesque's linguistic activity.

Anthropological Linguistics, 39 (1),60-73.

Brown, C.H. (1991). Hieroglyphic literacy in ancient

Mayaland: Inferences from linguistics data. Current

Anthropology, 32(4), 489-495.

Clark, J.E. , Pye, M.E. The Pacific coast and the Olmec

question. In J.E. Clark and M.E.Pye (Ed.) , Olmec

Art and Archaeology in MesoAmerica pp.217-251).

Washington, D.C.: National Art Gallery.

Clegg, L.H. (1975). Who were the first Americans?, The

Black Scholar, 7 (1), 32-41.

Coe, M. (1989). The Olmec Heartland: evolution of ideology

. In R.J. Sharer and D. C. Grove (Eds.), Regional

Perspectives on the Olmecs (pp.68-82). New York:

Cambridge University Press.

Carlson,D. and Van Gerven,D.P. (1979). Diffusion,

biological determinism and bicultural adaptation in

the Nubian corridor, American Anthropologist, 81, 561-

580.

Desplagnes, M. (1906). Deux nouveau cranes humains de cites

lacustres. L'Anthropologie, 17, 134-137.

Diehl, R. A., & Coe, M.D. (1995). "Olmec archaeology". In

In Jill Guthrie (Ed.), Ritual and Rulership, (pp.11-

25). The Art Museum: Princeton University Press.

Delafosse,M. "Vai leur langue et leur systeme d'ecriture",

L'Anthrpologie 10, 1899.

Dieterlen, G. (1957). Essai sur le religion bambara.

Presses Universitaire de France.

Drew, D. (1999) The lost chronicles of the Maya Kings. Los

Angeles: University of California Press.

DuBois, W.E.B. (1924). The Gift of Black Folks. Boston.

Gutherie, J. (ed.).(1995). The Olmec World: Ritual and

   rulership , Princeton University: The Art Museum.

Hau, K. (1973). Pre-Islamic writing in West Africa.

   Bulletin de l'Institut Fondamental Afrique Noire

   (IFAN), t 35, Ser. B number 1, 1-45.

Hau, K. (1978). African writing in the New World. Bull. de

   l'IFAN, t 40, Ser. B , number 1, 28-48.

Irwin,C.Fair Gods and Stone Faces.

Keita,S.O.Y. (1993). Studies and comments on ancient

   Egyptian biological relationships, History in Africa,

   20, 129-131.

Keita,S.O.Y.& Kittles,R.A. (1997). The persistence of
racial thinking

   and the myth of racial divergence, American
Anthropologist, 99

   (3), 534-544.

Jelinek, J. (1985). Tillizahren, the key site of the

   Fezzanese rock art, Anthropologie, 23(3), 223-275.

Landa, D. de. (1978). Yucatan before and after the

Conquest. (Trans. by) William Gates.New York: Dover

Publications.

Keita, S.O.Y. (1996) The diversity of indigenous Africans.
In Egypt in Africa, (ed.) Theodore Celenko (pp.104-
105). Bloomington, IN:Indianapolis Museum of Art and
Indiana University Press.

Landa, D. de. (1978). Yucatan before and after the
Conquest. (Trans. by) William Gates.
New York: Dover Publications.

Lawrence, H.G. (1962). African explorers of the New World,
The Crisis, 321-332.

Lhote, H. (1987). Les gravures du pourtour occidental et du
centre de l'Air. Editions Recherche sur les
Civilisation Memoire, No.70. Paris: CNRS.

MacGaffey,W.(1970). Concepts of race in Northeast Africa.
In J.D. Fage and R.A. Oliver, Papers in African
Prehistory (pp.99-115), Cambridge: Cambridge
University Press.

Marquez,C.(1956). Estudios arqueologicas y
ethnograficas .
Mexico.

McCall, D.P. (1971). The cultural map and time profile of

the Manding speaking people. In Paper on Manding,
(ed.) by D. Dalby (pp. 27-98).Bloomington: Indiana
University Press.

McIntosh, S.K. & McIntosh, R. (1979). Initial perspectives
on prehistoric subsistence in the Inland Niger Delta
(Mali), World Archaeology, 2 (2), 227-243.

McIntosh, S.K. & McIntosh, R. (1981). West African
Prehistory, American Scientist, 69, 602-613.

Morley, S.G., Brainerd, G.W. & Sharer, R.J. (1983). The
Ancient Maya. Stanford:Standford University Press.

Norman, G. (1976). Izapa Sculpture.

Navarrete, C. (1976). The Olmec rock carving at Pijijipan
Chiapas, Mexico and other Olmec Pieces, from Chiapas
and Guatemala. New World Archaeological Foundation, No.
35. Provo, Utah : Brigham Young University Press.

Pouligny, D. (1988). Les Olmeques. Archeologie, 12, p.194.

Rafineque, C. (1832). "Second letter to Mr. Champollion on
the Graphic systems of America and the glyphs of
Ololum [Mayan] of Palenque in central America-elements

of the glyphs", Atlantic Journal 1, (2) :44-45.

Sahagun, R. de. (1946). Historia General de las Casas de la

Nueva Espana. Mexico City: Editoria Nueva Espana.

Schele, L. & Freidel, D. (1990). A Forest of Kings. New

York: William Morrow and Company, Inc.

Smith, V.G. (1984). Izapa Relief Carving. Washington, D.C.:

Dumbarton Oaks Research Library and Collection.

Stross, B. (1973). Maya Hieroglyphic writing and Mixe-

Zoquean. Anthropological Linguistics, 24 (1), 73-134.

Tate, C. E. (1995). Art in Olmec Culture. In J Gutherie

(ed.), The Olmec World: Ritual and rulership (pp.45-

67) The Art Museum, Princeton

University.

Taylor, J.H. (1991). Egypt and Nubia. Cambridge, MA:

Harvard University Press.

Thompson, A.A. (1975). Pre-Columbian (African) presence in

the Western Hemisphere, <u>Negro History Bulletin</u>, 38
(7), 452-456.

Tozzer, A.M. (ed).(1941). <u>Relacion de las Casa de Yucatan.</u>

Peabody Museum of American Archaeology and Ethnology

,1941.

van Sertima, I. (1976). <u>They came before Columbus: The
African presence in ancient America</u>. New York: Random
House.

Underhill,P.A.,Jin,L., Zemans,R., Oefner,J and Cavalli-
Sforza,L.L.(1996, January). A pre-Columbian Y
chromosome-specific transition and its implications
for human evolutionary history, <u>Proceedings of the</u>
<u>National Academy of Science USA</u>,93, 196-200.

Van Rossum,P. (1996). Olmec skeletons African? No,
just poor   scholarship.

<u>http://copan.bioz.unibas.ch/meso/rossum.html</u>.

Von Wuthenau, Alexander. (1980). <u>Unexplained Faces in</u>
<u>Ancient America</u>, 2nd Edition, Mexico 1980.

Wiercinski, A.(1969). Affinidades raciales de algunas
poblaiones antiquas de Mexico, <u>Anales de INAH, 7a</u>
<u>epoca</u>, tomo II, 123-143.

Wiercinski,A. (1972). Inter-and Intrapopulational Racial

Differentiation of Tlatilco, Cerro de Las Mesas,

Teothuacan, Monte Alban and Yucatan Maya, XXXlX

Congreso Intern. de Americanistas, Lima 1970 ,Vol.1,

231-252.

Wiercinski,A. (1972b). An anthropological study on the

origin of "Olmecs", Swiatowit ,33, 143-174.

Wiercinski, A. & Jairazbhoy, R.A. (1975) "Comment", The New

Diffusionist,5 (18),5.

Winters, C.A. (1977). The influence of the Mande scripts on

American ancient writing systems. Bulletin de l'IFAN,

t.39, Ser.B ,Number 2, 405-431.

Winters, C.A.(1979). Manding writing in the New World--Part

1, Journal of African Civilization, 1 (1), 81-97.

Winters, C.A. (1980). Appendix B: The Jade Celts of

LaVenta. In A. von Wuthenau, Unexpected faces in

Ancient America (pp. 235-237). 2nd Edition. Mexico.

Winters, C.A. (December 1981/ January 1982). Mexico's Black

heritage, The Black Collegian,76-82.

Winters,C.A. (1983). "The ancient Manding script". I.

   Sertima (Ed.), Blacks in Science: ancient and modern,

   (ed.) by I. Sertima, (pp. 208-214), London:

   Transaction Books.

Winters, C.A. (1984a). Blacks in ancient America.

   Colorlines, 3(2), 27-28.

Winters, C.A. (1984b). Africans found first American

   Civilization, African Monitor, 1, 16-18.

Winters, C.A. (1986)."The Migration routes of the Proto-

   Mande",The Mankind Quarterly 27 (1), 77-96.

Winters, C.A. (1997, April). The decipherment of Olmec

   Writing. Paper presented at the 74th meeting of the

   Central States Anthropological Society, Milwaukee,

   Wis.

Wuthenau, A. von. (1980). Unexpected Faces in Ancient

   America. 2nd Edition. Mexico.

Zahn, D. (1974). The Bambara. Leiden: E.J. Brill.

END NOTES

_____

i.Robert S. Chamberlain, Francisco de Montejo and the Conquest of Mexico. Ph.D
Dissertation, Harvard University. 1936.

ii.Jose Melgar, "Antiguedades Mexicanas", Sociedad Mexicana de Geografica y
estadistica Boletin, 2a epoca I,(1869), pp.292-297.

iii.J. Soustelle, The Olmecs: The Oldest Civilization in Mexico, (Garden City, N.Y. :
Doubleday and Com., Inc., 1984) p.9.

iv.Matthew W. Stirling, "Discovering the New World's Oldest Dated, Work of Man",
National Geographic Magazine, vol. 76 (August 1939), pp.183-218.

v.Richard A. Diehl and Michael D. Coe, "Olmec Archaeology", in The Olmec World:
Ritual and Rulership, (ed.) by Jill Guthrie , (Princeton University: The Art Museum
1995) p.11.

vi. Thor Heyerdahl, The Ra Expeditions, (New York: New American Library, 1971)
p.61.

vii. Graves, p.44.

viii. Thor Heyerdahl, The Ra Expeditions, (New York: New American Library, 1971)
p.61.

ix. Graves, p.44.

x. Thor Heyerdahl, The Ra Expeditions, (New York: New American Library, 1971) p.61.

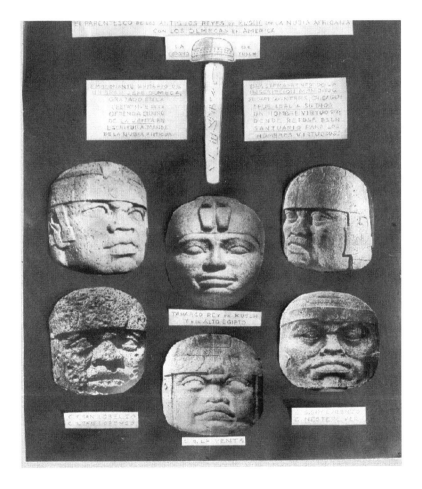

INDEX

Made in the USA
Lexington, KY
13 October 2013